Contents

Part 1

Bereavement means a significant loss; realising the loss; mourning; shock; numbness; rejection; denial and disbelief; longing; loss; searching; anger, bitterness and hate; anxiety and fear; guilt and shame; reminiscing and remembering; depression; murder and thoughts of; considerations of suicide; blame, forgiveness and letting go.

Part 2

Some Of The Causes And Their Effects

The beginning; baby is born; late diagnosis; being told; reactions; telling others; early effects on the family; the next stages; first separations; services and support; friends and family; growing up; looking back; looking forward.

Some attitudes and beliefs; living a lie; before knowing; finding out; what was the reality?; what is there to do?; deciding to stay; deciding to split.

Part 3

Effects On Others

Part 4

What has been lost? What do I have? What can I do with it? What has been gained?

Preface

After suffering from a bereavement without a death, I gained the awareness of how different these things look, feel and are, before and after they happen. I also discovered that much of what I had felt, experienced and had to deal with, were only slightly reflected in most books about bereavement. From these things came the initial reason for writing this book.

The ideas in this book have gradually grown and taken shape over a number of years, as I talked to many people who have been willing to share their stories, feelings, hopes and fears.

To all of these I wish to express my gratitude, without them this book could not possibly have been written. To all those who have supported and encouraged me in so many ways, thank you.

Introduction

We cannot see the child before he is conceived, we cannot see into the hearts and minds of friends and those we love and we cannot see the many twists and turns our life will take. Therefore there will be times for all of us when things are not or do not turn out to be what we hoped for, expected or wanted.

I often think about the time when, as a young social worker, I looked down at the tiny Down's Syndrome baby in the hospital crib and hoped that her parents would accept her and take her home. I wondered then what I would do in their situation, I hoped that I would take mine home. I never dreamed that I would have the opportunity to find out.

As I write this, I am watching out for the mini-bus bringing my teenage, Down's Syndrome son home from school. How different it all looks from this position; the problems, the joys, the sorrows and the effect it has all had on so many lives.

Having had further opportunities to experience things that I believed would 'never happen to me', the questions without answers, confusion at the lack of reason, feelings of helplessness and hopelessness. Wondering what was happening to me, in me, around me and why? The questions piled up, what should I do, walk away or stay? Show my true feelings and face the risks? Am I a victim or did I allow this to happen?

When we try to help, comfort and support those who are distressed, whether they are relatives, friends, or we are in the role of professional helper, the questions are likely to be much the same and we have to cope with our own feeling as well as theirs. Trying to comfort someone who is coping with loss, we often experience a mixture of feelings, from helplessness to anger, concern to irritation, then guilt for not acting or feeling as we would like to or that we feel we should.

The particular situation may be unusual or not, but this is no measure of the pain, distress and confusion that is caused. It can be very painful to be 'dumped' by a girl or boy friend. If you are young, many of those around will be unsympathetic, considering it just part of 'growing up', even though the pain and distress can be great enough for suicide to be attempted.

Many of the feelings associated with having a child with a learning disability, are shared by the families of many other children who are considered 'different', because of a disability. This may be due to many things such as cerebral palsy, achondroplasia (dwarfism), deafness or some form of disfigurement.

It is devastating for parents to discover that their child has 'dropped out' or become a drug addict, or that they have done things or behaved in ways that the parents, if not the rest of society find unacceptable.

When we marry we may believe that we have some idea about the person we are marrying but many people discover that this is not so. Not only in the ways I have discussed in this book and the general things that we learn about each other, but in ways that have an enormous impact on lives, such as discovering that a partner is a transvestite or that they wish to change their sex.

We also often believe that we know where our life is heading, but sometimes due to a change in our partner, things are not or do not turn out the way we expected. It can be hard for someone such as, the wife of a rich business man, who enjoys a certain lifestyle, to suddenly find he wishes to give it all up and run a croft in Scotland, or that he feels called from his present way of life to become a priest.

The life that was expected has gone, the way of life will change considerably, as will those involved. There will be many feelings, doubts and uncertainties to cope with, as well as decisions to be made about where they stand and what they are going to do, how to cope with the changes that will have to be faced whether they go with them or not.

Each person will see and feel their loss, or the loss faced by another person differently. How it is viewed and coped with will depend on many things including, how many losses there have been in the past and what is being coped with at present. We are also affected by the way we viewed this particular loss when it happened to someone in the past, but probably the most important thing is the emotional and physical support that is available.

If the loss has happened to someone else, we need to be aware of how much it has affected us and how we are dealing with it. We need to consider how much help and support they need, how much we are willing and able to help and what is the best way of doing this.

It would not be possible to discuss every cause and effect but I do not feel that this is necessary or necessarily helpful. What is true for one is often not true for another, what one person feels in a situation someone else would feel in another.

I have looked at situations which happen to people all the time, so often that unless we are personally affected, it is easy to be unfeeling. This is not helped by the tabloid press who present many of these things as more of a circus than a heart-break.

It is easy to look at someone else and believe that we would handle things differently or never have allowed it to happen in the first place. If it is happening to us we often believe that we should be dealing with it differently or should have prevented it happening.

The fact is that because these things are so common, we think that we know about them and what we, or others should do. We may believe for example, that if our husband had an affair we would just kick him out, I have even heard people say that they would be relieved. There are many who believe that if their child was born with a disability they would just love and accept it and carry on, whilst others feel that they would just not cope.

Some will consider that a mild learning disability is not too much of a problem, whilst someone else will feel that it is a tragedy. Some cope with their partner cross-dressing whilst another person cannot deal with it at all. Your child having a sexual partner may not be a problem but it may be a different matter if they are the same sex, a different colour, religion or there is a big difference in age.

The only thing for certain is that we do not know for certain how we will react or what we will do, whether it has happened to someone else or to ourselves we will find out more about ourselves. We may be weaker or stronger, more open-minded or prejudiced, more or less able to change our understanding or see things from another person's viewpoint.

There are many people who have suffered loss and live to regret hasty decisions made whilst they were in the early stages of grief. Many relationships have been damaged and families torn apart by words or actions. Many have taken their own lives or become addicted to alcohol or drugs because they and those involved were not aware of the effect of the loss both within themselves and others.

PART 1

GRIEF

When there is a bereavement without a death,
we not only grieve for what we have lost,
but are likely to become lost in grief for what we have.

GRIEF

Bereavement means a significant loss

It is not only the death of someone close to us that causes us grief, it can be caused by any major loss in our lives. We may be surprised by the strength of the feelings that we have or that others are experiencing.

It may be that this loss is enormous, it may be that this loss has caused other unresolved grief to surface and cause the pain. There is no gain in measuring the loss, either our own or that of another person. Each situation is different and is perceived and felt as different by each person. We should never assume how another feels, for example: the death of a parent may be a totally shattering experience to a loved child but to an abused child it may bring relief, healing and security. The meaning of any loss is different for each individual.

This is true for other losses, for example, a child may be born with a severe learning disability or have an illness or accident resulting in the same, a loved partner may have an affair or leave, or a parent or partner develop Alzheimer's Disease. These losses may be sudden and unexpected or we may have suspected what was wrong, but when we are actually told it can be overwhelming. Instead of coming to terms with life without the deceased person, here it is necessary to come to terms with the loss of the person that was or the person who you believed they were, the normal child you were expecting or the loving, faithful partner you believed you had. At the same time, learning to develop an acceptance of and a relationship with the person who is there. A person who you do not know or understand, a baby who is handicapped, someone who is a liar and a cheat, or someone who is changing from a loving, competent, caring mother into a dependent, confused stranger.

The pain and grief of the loss have to be worked through, before there can be acceptance and healing. If this is not achieved there will be problems of unresolved grief that continue to cause us difficulties in the form of physical symptoms, depression, maladaptive behaviour or many other problems that are associated with unresolved grief.

The pain and grief are often not recognised by others and often people have to deal with this alone and unsupported, not understanding what is happening to them and being misunderstood or having their feelings belittled by those around them.

The significance of what has been lost may not always be recognised even by the person who has experienced the loss. We may believe or be convinced by others that it is not really all that serious,

"After all it is not as though someone has died",

"There are plenty more fish in the sea".

"You are better off without him".

"You have been specially chosen".

There is plenty of encouragement to get on with life, "these things happen all the time". This makes it difficult to see and appreciate the enormity of what has happened and allow our grief the time it needs to be properly resolved. This is true whether we are the one who is suffering or someone who is looking on and perhaps wondering how to help.

Because something happens quite often, like a marriage breakdown, many people do not realise that this may be worse than the death of the partner. To be rejected because another person or way of life is preferable; to lose the life that you had known and often even the home you had; to have to continue to have contact with the person, to negotiate the splitting up of everything when none of this is your choice, can be so painful it can even lead to suicide.

Whatever the loss, life can never be the same. It may be some time before we are aware of all the things that have changed and what we have to give up. Whether it is a partner who has left or a child has been diagnosed as handicapped, the family will not be as it was or how we expected it to be in the future.

These differences will probably be most noticeable at times like Christmas, when there may be no family, or it may be that one member may not be able to join in or will prevent the rest of the family from having the sort of Christmas they would have had. Holidays may not be afforded anymore or have to be geared to one member of the family or that member has to be excluded to give everyone else a break. Everyday life has to change to an extent that it would not have, had the loss not happened. These changes are made all the more painful to deal with as they are forced upon us with as much choice and control as we have over death.

When people die they stay the same to us or we can choose to remember them as they were. The memories are carried within us, we grieve for what we have lost. When what we have lost is not the physical person but the person as they were or we believed they were. We grieve for what we have, often unaware of the pain of the loss and the need to grieve for this. Until we have mourned for the loss, we cannot deal with what we have.

Sometimes we are unaware of what we have lost or why we are feeling so bad when it was our choice or what we wanted for a long time. There may be a long period of grieving even after a partner has been forced to leave. Any initial feelings of euphoria may not last for long. There may be grief for the loss of the relationship and life that should have been, feelings of guilt that the time together was a waste and feelings of failure. An acceptance of what has been and the future that is to be, can take a long time to achieve.

We may have to begin to learn to do things on our own, to cope on our own and manage things we have never had to before, the same as though a partner has died. If there are children we will probably still have to work with them, arrange access visits, agree what to do about money and belongings and help to take apart what we had. Even where this includes a lot of relief there is usually a lot of sadness and regret if only for the life that should have been. These feelings can come as an enormous shock when only relief was expected.

If there are children involved there is likely to be difficult behaviour to be dealt with. This can be caused in the child by the condition that has been diagnosed or from children trying to come to terms with what has happened in their lives. This may be the breakdown of their parents' marriage, having a handicapped sibling or coping with a confused relative.

Each of these events and at times there are more than one at a time, all make enormous demands on the family, threatening or removing its stability thereby removing the child's security. It is therefore not surprising that children may be difficult.

Caring parents feel pulled in all directions, trying to work out and balance priorities, to give time, attention and understanding when required. Their own needs may at times be so overwhelming that for at least a while they may be unable to think of or deal with anything in a reasonable or even safe manner. This can lead to even more guilt and stress.

In this society we find it difficult enough to know how to deal with relatives and friends of someone who has died. At least in death there are the rituals of the funeral, flowers and condolences notices are placed in the papers and it is generally accepted that time will be taken off work. These things enable people to get together to show their support and sympathy, they mark the passing of the deceased, they have gone totally out of our lives forever.

Where the bereavement does not have a death, there are no services or rituals, no way of people coming together to share their grief or show their love and support. Family and friends may not even know anything has happened, they may have to decide whose fault it is and whose side they are on. The end is often hard to mark, is it an end or is it just continuing but different?

Realising the loss

When someone dies, they have gone from this life forever. The fact that they are not coming back is marked in many ways and we are given opportunities to say 'goodbye'. For some people it is important to see the dead body, the funeral is another opportunity and marks the end of a way of life and the beginning of a new one. It is a time for family and friends to get together to show their love, support and caring for the bereaved.

It is very hard for the bereaved to realise that the deceased will not need their clothes and possessions any longer and that they will not be there anymore. Life will continue without them.

The task of the bereaved, where there has been a death, is to face and accept the loss. They will go through a period of mourning whilst they come to terms with a life without the deceased person. They must begin to build a new life and find other people and ways in which to reinvest their emotional energies. This letting go of the deceased person does not mean that the bereaved has got over the loss or has discarded the past, it means that they now know that they are able to move on and can take the love and memories they have with them.

Where someone has not died, but we have experienced a great loss it is difficult to think of our loss in terms of bereavement. It is therefore not surprising that we are often unaware of what is happening to our emotions and feelings. It may seem indecent to mourn for a person who has not died and is in fact still with us. How do we say 'goodbye' and to what or who do we say it? There are many things that contribute to the difficulties and confusion, for example; the feeling that where there is life there is hope can keep us in a state of suspended animation for a long time, denying us the opportunity to say 'goodbye' to what was. This can be fuelled by others, sometimes purposefully, such as when a partner keeps promising that you will be together again or by relatives who insist that the truth be denied as they cannot face it themselves. At other times there is a lack of information, such as when it is necessary to wait over a long period to see how much an ill child will recover.

If we can accept that we are separated and that he is not coming back, the awareness of our bereavement can disappear under the feelings of rejection and the difficulties of working out a new relationship, contact, belongings, finance and children. The clothes and possessions are still needed only not here. Even if no further contact is foreseen, who knows if a meeting may happen by chance, this may be a dread that is lived with for years.

After discovering a partner has had an affair they can never again be the same person to us and the relationship will never be the same, but the fact of bereavement and the mourning for our loss can be denied in the effort to put things back together. How do you say 'goodbye' to someone you are making a new life with?

A baby who has been diagnosed as having Down's Syndrome is the person he always was, only no-one knew, He is also still here. Rather than leaving a space in my life he will be in my life needing me, for the rest of my life. How can I possibly say 'goodbye'?

Mourning

I feel that it is important to first look at what we mean when we talk about mourning. When someone says that a separation or having a handicapped child is just like a bereavement, this is true, even if it is only part of the picture. It is generally accepted that we all go through certain stages, feelings and emotions when we are coming to terms with a loss. It is important to understand what is happening to us, to know that often what we are feeling is not only normal and reasonable, under the circumstances, but can be a sign of health and progress.

It can be shocking and distressing to find that we have feelings that are unexpected and unacceptable to us. We can feel that we are going mad and wonder what is happening.

You may feel that you are turning into a horrible person if for example you are angry with your baby for being handicapped. It is horrible to feel that we are pathetic, stupid and bad if we admit even to ourselves that we long to be held by someone who has lied, cheated or even abused us. Many of us live with feelings of guilt and shame for what someone else has done, even though we may not be to blame in any way.

How can we talk to anyone about these feelings if we feel that we are bad or unacceptable for having them. It is very important that we realise that these feelings are normal and are in fact necessary and understandable. They are an essential part of coming to terms with our loss so that we are able to move on.

Although these feelings are written about in a particular order, this is not necessarily the order or way that anyone will go through them. The way ahead will at times be far from straight forward, we may go back for a while to what we had already dealt with or what we felt that we had.

Any of these feelings may be just fleeting. One person may only suffer from a state of shock for a few seconds before other emotions rush in and take over, someone else may collapse or be unable to respond for some time. Another person may feel very angry and bitter, rightly or wrongly blaming others for what has happened. They may even become stuck here for a long time. Yet another person may avoid this by not becoming angry but depressed. These feelings cannot be avoided or denied. If they are not dealt with they will continue to affect out lives in different ways; by bursting out in inappropriate anger, by descending on us in bouts of depression, over-dependence on alcohol or an inability to find happiness or contentment in our lives.

Everyone's loss is different. We all deal very differently with what has happened to us, depending on the loss, our own background, how expected or unexpected it is and the care and support that we receive. In whatever way we do it, we all share and have to work through these feelings, each in our own way, when we deal with losses in our life.

Shock

This is what happens when we suddenly realise what has really happened. It is a mental, physical and emotional reaction and its effect can vary from very little response to total collapse. It can feel like a stunning blow or being frozen like a block of ice. The effect may last for a few seconds or a much longer time.

What we have just discovered, like any bereavement may be sudden and totally unexpected, it may be something that we had been denying for some time or it may be something that was suspected but there had been hope of a different outcome. Now we are hit by the facts and the reality, any final hope has been ripped away.

How we are given this information or find out what the truth is can have a significant effect on the long-term recovery of the bereaved and future relationships. For some, it is a doctor in his office giving a diagnosis as kindly and gently as possible, giving time for the news to sink in a bit, explaining as much as possible and giving the opportunity for another meeting when the shock has receded. For another it may be that the diagnosis accidentally slips out in a totally unsuitable situation.

Other losses may be put to us gently or we may discover evidence which makes us realise with sudden shock the true situation that we are facing and have to deal with.

Numbness

Often there is an initial cutting off from our feelings. There is a sense of unreality, of not being connected or involved. We are not switched on to our feelings, what is happening around us and we feel cocooned from the world.

Our actions may be automatic, decision making may be difficult or our thoughts may be quite clear, decisions are made, everything is seen and remembered but the feelings are not there. Life may have a dreamlike or nightmarish quality, with a wish to wake up and get back to life as it was, the fact that this now is the reality is too painful to bear.

Often at this time there is pressure to make decisions, but unless it is a matter of life and death these should be put off. Making decisions should be avoided, because they may well be regretted later, there may also so be a lot of anger and resentment towards those who encouraged us to make decisions when we were in no state to make them. It is no time to make a long term decision of what to do with a handicapped child or a confused parent. With feelings and emotions in shut down, it is a 'quiet time' when partners may try to put pressure on us to make long term decisions about such matters as access, finance, housing and divorce.

Rejection

As we come out of shock what has happened begins to touch us. We do not want to believe or face what has happened and may deny it, refusing to believe that things are the way they are or we reject the idea, the person or the messenger and refuse to accept them.

One of the most obvious forms of rejection is where a handicapped baby is born and the parents reject it and refuse to take it home. Another is where a partner who has had an affair may be immediately thrown out of their home. Such decisions as these may be the right ones in the long term or they may not be, but there is a good chance that a decision made in this way will be regretted or leave many unanswered questions in the future.

At this stage feelings may seem very firm and definite but they are an immediate emotional response to what has happened. Later when things are calmer and there has been an opportunity to come to terms with the loss, there may be the possibility of making a new relationship with the person who is there.

It is necessary for time, support and information to be given to the bereaved so that they can begin to come to terms with what has happened, see it in a wider context, look at the consequences of various actions and then to be able to make an informed decision. This is not the time to put pressure on to the bereaved to make long term firm decisions, but all too often this is what happens. Pressure is put on, by relatives, hospitals, social workers and others for a decision to be made.

Rejection may be of the diagnosis or the information that has been given. This may just be disbelief or strenuous efforts made to prove that this is not true. Sometimes the rejection is of the messenger, the doctor who gives the bad news, the hospital or the friend who believed that you had the right to know what was happening.

Denial and disbelief

If someone has died, however difficult and painful this may be, it is an irreversible fact. Where there has not been a death, the fact of the loss may not be obvious and it may be a long time before it is realised or admitted. Very often we live in a state of denial as a conscious or subconscious way of avoiding facing a painful truth. Somewhere inside we know that if we admit the truth to ourselves, it will be very painful, we may have to make choices or decisions that will change our life forever.

This denial may even go on for many years until we are forced to see the truth. Later we wonder how we could not have known and blame ourselves for our stupidity. Often we realise that we had in fact known but denied that things were not right, convinced ourselves that the problems were due to something like 'pressure of work'.

If a child is not making progress we say that 'all children are different' and concentrate on what he can do. The experiences of other people often show us that all is probably well and we are reassured by others who tell us not to worry. We grasp this and hold on, it is what we want to believe and it enables us to deny the truth.

There are times when the denial comes from another person, for example, a partner who is having an affair may well deny this is happening. Many parents of special needs children have been told that there is nothing wrong with their child they are just neurotic or bad parents.

It is very difficult to find the truth within ourselves or in the other person. I ask myself am I being honest with myself, am I just being over anxious or am I lying to myself because I do not want to face the truth. Is the other person right, being honest, or just defending themselves. There are times when denial from the other person involves an attack on our own trust, honesty and integrity. Later when we are proved to be right it is a very bitter pill to swallow and very difficult to forgive or leave behind.

Later, whilst working through our grief, we very often see this time whilst the truth was being denied by ourselves or others as wasted. We were living a lie, living as though life was one way when in fact it was another and making plans for a future based on that lie.

We are aware that very often whilst we were unaware of what was happening, others could see it and we can only guess at their thoughts and comments. But very few people would have been thanked for making us face up to what we are denying. A son who tells his parents he is gay may be wanting his parents to see and share in his real life. But although his parents may have been aware that this is the case, they might find it totally unacceptable and be unable to deal with the reality, at least for a long time.

When there is a bereavement without a death, usually the person is still there, looking the same, whilst our life has been shattered. It is all to easy to forget for a while, to slip back into how it was, to hold on to a belief that things will return to normal when this has all passed.

Longing

The turbulent feelings are very hard to cope with, many emotions are jumbled together and there is often a very big difference between what our rational brain is telling us and the thoughts and feelings that we are having. We know when we cannot have something and that it may even be bad for us if we did but that does not stop us longing.

Feeling like this can make us feel stupid and irrational. It is understandable to long for our baby to be normal and life to be ordinary again but it is more difficult to admit even to ourselves that we long to be back with a person who has hurt us very badly. This is something that family and friends who care about us can find very difficult to understand, accept and help us to deal with.

When someone dies there is often a longing to see the person, even if it is just once more, to touch or be held again. The fact that these longings cannot be fulfilled is so very painful, but it makes us face the reality of what has happened. Comfort may be found in the fact that the one who died did not want to leave and would give us love and comfort if they could.

For someone who has been deserted, the other person chose to leave and the longings are denied by that person. In other situations the person is still there, looking the same but the longing is for the person they were before and things to be the same as they were.

These feelings of longing can be overwhelming. If they are not worked through they can lead us back again to suffer the same hurts from either the same person or someone similar. Many people dream for a while of what might be, however unlikely. Some fulfill their longings for a few moments by sleeping with their ex-partner. The longings can lead us across the globe looking for a cure and can cause us to reject those who do not agree with and support us.

We yearn for what we have lost, we grieve for what we have. We feel helpless, all our best efforts have come to nothing or even worse we have been rejected as worth nothing. We may well be feeling stripped of self respect and the respect and understanding of others.

It is at this time that those who love and care for us find it very difficult to cope with us and their own feelings as they see us being unrealistic, heading for more hurt, prolonging the agony and their own sympathy and patience disappearing. Their over-view may give them a clearer picture of the possible pitfalls ahead, which they should gently share with us. We must make sure that though we may not deal with this stage in the best way, we do not remain here, but continue to move forward.

Loss

When we have lost someone we love, but not through death, there is always the possibility, however slight that it may not be final. Some couples get back together, sometimes after many years. Relationships survive affairs, sometimes they appear to be better than before and even if a baby is diagnosed as having a problem, there is still a baby to be cared for and loved. We hang on to the hope that it is not true, if it is then it will turn out to be alright, or not that bad, but whatever the outcome, we will eventually have to realise that we have been bereaved and face the loss of what we had.

What we have lost is the person we had or thought we had, we now know that things have changed or were never as we thought they were. Once we know something we can never un-know it, what we now know has changed our life, we have lost the life and relationship that we had. There has been a loss of trust. Self-esteem and self-confidence have probably taken a nose dive and so much that we valued, worked hard for and thought we had, has gone.

The past is called into question, are these the rewards for working hard and being good. Was our past the way we thought or is what really happened somewhat different? So many beliefs that we may not even have realised we held, which made the world feel a safer place for us, are shattered. Beliefs such as; my marriage will be for always, doctors and hospitals make people better, these things happen to other people, they must have done something to deserve the bad things that happened to them. When these bad things happen to us we lose the security but do not lose these implied criticisms which we now level at ourselves and are aware that others will be levelling at us.

It may be very difficult to have any confidence in the future, which may look bleak and empty and the feelings we have are of futility. If all that can be seen is failure and a belief that everything attempted has gone or will go wrong, it is very hard to start again. Faith in those around us may be lost and for many their God has failed them or is punishing them, maybe for some unknown or imagined wrong they have done.

Life as we knew it, planned it and expected it to be has been lost, so has our trust in a lot of things and people. It is hardly surprising that all too often this can lead to other losses such as loss of self respect, alcohol, tobacco or drug abuse, loss of health and sometimes loss of life.

One of the big losses is an ordinary life, we may not have thought much about it when we had it and we may even have hated it. What we wanted was interest and excitement, not this. We miss just being part of a couple, just getting on with life without wondering what is going on behind our back, just having a child who goes off to school with the other kids.

Often so much of what was taken for granted has gone, freedom is restricted and there is no end in sight. Society wants you to be wonderful and cope, help is probably in short supply, it is assumed that you are being helped out with benefits, taxis to school and such like, so people believe that you are being 'looked after'.

To cope with the pain of loss, the grief and emptiness, we need time and space. Time to grieve, time to disappear into ourselves to find the strength to cope, time to find our balance, time and the opportunity to talk to others to enable us to work through our grief.

Unfortunately what we usually have also lost is time and space. The person has not died, there is no space, frequently there is less – less time, less space, less money. The time and space are taken up with hospital appointments and development programmes, or coping on your own and doing what had previously been done by two, often coping at the same time with distressed and confused children.

Money that had been running one home has to run two when a relationship breaks down, so there will be less. If you have become a carer it may mean someone is unable to work or has to work less so there is less income. Breaks, space and quality of life are lost.

Searching

If we lose something we search for it but first we have to be aware that we have lost something and what it is that we have lost.

Most of us have at one time or another had the feeling that we have forgotten something or that something is missing. We stop and think about it and realise what it is, maybe we did not finish a job we started or our youngest child has started school and we miss having a little one constantly with us. Having worked it out we can get on with our life.

Sometimes we do not know what is making us unsettled, we move from place to place, looking for the something that will make us feel better. When we have been bereaved but no one has died, it may be very difficult to realise that we are looking for the lost one and the life we have lost. What we are doing is searching.

Mostly we search and find the one we have but it is not the one we are looking for, we search for what we had so that it can be put back in its place, or where we know where it is. We search for the way to make everything fine and as it should be again, to feel comfortable in ourselves again.

We may do this by looking for a cure or someone to tell us that a mistake has been made and everything is alright. We search for ways to make our children with learning disabilities normal, not only keep them up to par but become better than others. We search for ways to get someone back, of making ourselves different or changing their minds.

In our search we may find and link up with others who have had the same experiences, either as individuals or part of a group. Those on the same journey can give us support, we can share experiences and learn from one another.

Until we realise that we have lost something and what it is, we cannot accept the loss of it from our life or come to terms with what this means for us and put our efforts into moving forward.

Anger, bitterness and hate

It is normal to feel angry when we have been hurt. To feel anger, hate and bitterness towards those who have hurt us, whether it is their fault or not. Anger at ourselves for what has happened and the way we are feeling. Anger at other people, God and life itself.

As in so many areas of the grieving process, what is wrong or right, reasonable or unreasonable, is very difficult to see or work out. Often this is not the point, we are overwhelmed by our feelings which are often far from reasonable or rational

When someone dies we feel angry at them for leaving us, even though they did not have a choice. It is therefore understandable if we feel angry at someone who has chosen to leave, to feel angry at our baby who is handicapped because we are hurt by his disability, angry at ourselves as we should not have let this happen, angry at doctors, family and friends. We also become angry at ourselves for feeling angry.

We feel bitter at the unfairness of life, about the opportunities we have lost and what we have been left with. We can feel bitterness, not only towards those who have hurt us but towards those who do not understand or we feel are better off than us, particularly if we do not feel that they deserve or appreciate it.

We cannot help the feelings we have, but we can choose to respond to them or not. If we deny our feelings they will be bottled up and cause us problems later. Feelings of anger are no exception, the feelings need to be worked through and resolved, many feelings will disappear when they are looked at. Feelings of anger can be very frightening both in ourselves and in others, we may be frightened of our feelings and impulses, ashamed of them, feel guilty, confused or become depressed.

Feelings of hate and anger, are held on to with absolute determination by some people. They feel that somehow, by letting these feelings go, they are letting the one who hurt them off the hook. What they fail to realise is that it is themselves they are punishing. Whilst we carry these feelings we are allowing the other person to continue to have control over our feelings and actions, by carrying the hate of them in us, we are keeping them with us.

When we can truly say: this person has caused me enough grief and misery, they will no longer have any influence or effect on my life I can let them go. We then know that we are free to feel, free to take control of and get on with our own life. Whilst we are hanging on to our feelings about them, we are hanging on to them.

If we deny our hatred and anger, it does not go away, it may ooze out in irritability and intolerance or it may be hidden under tight control. We have often been brought up to believe that it is wrong to be angry, bitter or hate people, particularly if they cannot help what they are doing. We see it as a bad thing to be angry at a disabled or confused person as they are not able to help what they are doing, but we would understand a parent feeling angry if a baby has a dirty nappy immediately after it has been changed and dressed.

We are allowed to be human and the same human emotions apply, we should not beat ourselves up with guilt for feeling what it is natural to feel. What we need is to accept and deal with our feelings so that they do not need to be denied and bottled up until they explode out of our control or cause us to become depressed.

It is most likely that there are many real causes and justifications for our anger. Although we may not be able to change what has happened, by directing our anger we may be able to use it to demand justice, an investigation, fund raise or start a support group.

It is essential for us to look at and face our feelings, to work through them so that one day we will be able to feel the feelings we want to; feelings of happiness, freedom and love.

Anxiety and fear

We become anxious when we become unsure of ourselves, other people and things around us. A certain amount of anxiety is normal, reasonable and at times helpful. For example, a little anxiety before exams will make us work, revise and prepare for them. With no anxiety we do not bother, we tell ourselves it will be alright or it does not matter.

If we become over anxious we panic, cannot think, cannot function and may become ill. If we do very badly in one exam, we are likely to become more anxious about the next. If we do badly in a lot of them, we may believe that we are stupid and cannot manage. We become depressed, stop trying and give up or we blame others such as our teachers or we decide that the tester did not like us, that they were unfair, so we become angry.

How we as individuals cope with exams is different to some people and the same as others. The same applies to how we cope with other difficult situations, it is easier to understand some people and their reactions than it is others.

To cope with life without becoming too anxious we need to believe that all will be well. Although we know that bad things can happen we do not spend our time expecting it. Most of those who tell us that they always expect the worst are kidding themselves. They may be attempting to prepare themselves but if what they say is true, they would not be able to function.

For example, when expecting a baby we believe it will be normal even though we know that this is not always so. When members of our family go out, we expect them to return safely. We believe that our children are at school and our partner is at work or wherever they tell us they will be. We buy Christmas presents and expect the recipients to be there to give them to, we plan and book our summer holidays in the winter and do not expect to use the insurance.

When we are bereaved, our whole world is turned upside down, suddenly our confidence in life has been shattered. Who or what can we trust anymore, if this bad thing can happen so might something else. So much is not as it seemed and it is difficult to know who or what to trust. Many of those who we thought were our friends or we thought we knew well are not what they seemed. We are avoided, misunderstood and hurt by comments made, many of which were supposed to be helpful or comforting.

Many people feel that they have avoided bad things happening to them and their families, by working hard, being good, and doing all the things they should. When something bad happens they not only feel hurt that this is the reward for their effort but they also feel very anxious because there is nothing more they can do to make sure they are safe.

How can we trust people or situations any more? How can we believe that anything we plan will be alright? What is going to go wrong next? Am I being told the truth? Suddenly we have to really face the fact that there are no guarantees and see how little in this life is certain.

All of this creates a high level of anxiety and we become very insecure. Tasks that had previously been carried out without hardly a thought suddenly become huge. We become very tired, there is often a return of childhood or other fears like fear of the dark or being alone.

We can feel that we will be overwhelmed by the feelings of anxiety and panic as we begin to look at the enormity of what has happened, what this means and what we have to face and deal with. If we are responsible for children then at the same time we have to help them to cope, calm their fears and anxieties. While dealing with our own anxiety about what has happened, we have to deal with how it is affecting them and their long term security.

We have the anxiety of coping with new situations, often not knowing anyone to whom this has happened before. What is wrong or right, good or bad. What are the answers? What am I supposed to do? How do you deal with a disabled baby? What do you do with it? What is the best way to help it? How do you cope on your own, divide up a home, share the kids?

It is hardly surprising then that we are anxious and fearful. We will need many new skills as we head into the unknown of our new life. When we have travelled a short distance down this road, then stop and look, we will probably realise that though we have learned a few new skills, we probably already possessed most of those we needed.

In fact, less has changed than we thought but now we know that there are few certainties in life and we are forced to really admit that we do not know what is going to happen in the future this may well be our greatest anxiety and challenge. We have to learn to relax and learn that our fears and anxieties do not have to rule us.

Guilt and shame

We do not have to have done anything wrong to feel guilt or shame, just as not all those who have done something wrong feel it.

The problem is often the view held by ourselves or society in general about whether anyone is to blame and if so who. When something bad happens to us we lose the protection of believing that these things happen to other people. We have suddenly become 'other people' and take on to ourselves, all that we previously thought of them.

If something goes wrong we usually believe that someone is to blame and all too often believe that the person must be ourselves. We work very hard to blame ourselves, to believe that we are being punished for something bad that we have done, either recently, as a child or perhaps in a previous life. The guilt and shame that we feel when we believe that we are a bad person is a very heavy burden, but for many people to understand and believe that they are not a bad person or that they are not to blame is even harder to deal with.

It is sometimes difficult to understand that it is not just an easy matter of cause and effect; I am being punished therefore I must have been bad, it has happened to her so she must have done something wrong. The fact that life is not fair and bad things can happen to anyone is hard to accept and can make us feel very insecure. It is far more comfortable and secure to feel that if something has happened to someone they are somehow to blame, they must have done something wrong, so that if I do not do anything wrong I will be safe. If bad things just happen to people, how can I be safe from these things happening to me?

On the other hand, if we can fully realise that bad things can happen without us being to blame, then we do not need to feel guilty or ashamed of what has happened. This is an area where the support of a trusted person can help us to look more clearly and objectively at the situation and our role in it. Have I been bad or unreasonable? Could I have foreseen or done anything about what has happened? Could I have done anything differently?

If in fact we have been bad, feeling guilt and remorse can make us think about the things that have happened and realise what we have done, then we can commit ourselves to changing, so that we do not create the situation again for ourselves or others. We must learn from our mistakes and move on. We cannot turn back the clock, we cannot change what has happened, but we can change ourselves.

Reminiscing and remembering

The past with its memories is the road we have travelled to get where we are now. It is usually necessary for the bereaved to talk about the circumstances, which led to their bereavement, to go over the past to sort out mixed up feelings and emotions. To look at the how, why, and what and to see if anything could have been done, so that things could have turned out differently.

Where there has been a death, the remembering will often be in the form of reminiscing, by looking at our past we can understand our relationship and allow the deceased to become part of us. The love and memories they have given are ours to keep, no one can take it away from us, they will always live in our hearts and minds. Their death may have been a waste, but not their life.

Where there has not been a death it is the life that has been, which may seem to be a total waste. Looking at a disabled child and remembering when they were well, does not bring us comfort. Remembering happy times in a marriage cannot bring us closer to the one who is gone, when we, along with our closeness and memories have been rejected.

On the road we have travelled we have learned and grown, our remembering is part of the journey. Our remembrances may be painful and may never become comforting but they are necessary steps on the road to healing and acceptance. When we have achieved this we can let go of anger and bitterness and begin to lay down the memories which will bring to us and those we love, comfort, in the future.

Depression

Depression is very often a reaction to a long period of stress or too much stress. Often we have managed to keep going whilst the going was tough but sink into depression as soon as the pressure is off. Whilst we were busy there was no time to think, consider the future or the full implications of what was happening. Now we have space and cannot avoid it.

A depression is often a sign that we need to change and move on. Old ways of thinking and being are no longer serving us well and it is necessary to find new ones. Avoiding the problem, attempting to get rid of it or running away from it does not help in the long term. It is necessary to work our way through the problems, to emerge at the other side willing, able and content to get on with our life.

By successfully negotiating the changes in our life, we grow and become stronger. To do this we have to give up outdated thoughts and ways of being, we have to change and adapt. Each time we grow and change as well as gaining, we have to lose something, leave something behind. Often we try to resist change, we want things to stay the same, or we do not want the discomfort of learning new ways. Change is also scary and carries risks with it. Life will never be the same again. We are even more likely to resist if the changes are forced upon us.

When we were young we were more likely to embrace the new, for example, we have to accept the fact of getting older. When we were young this was exciting, we waited impatiently to be old enough to do whatever the next step was, even though it was a bit scary. The loss of the safety and security of home was probably even seen as a bonus. As we get older, getting older is not so easily accepted. When we are facing our children growing up and leaving home, our looks becoming at best 'comfortable', we may well feel that the gains of growth and maturity do not compensate for our losses.

The losses in our life give us an opportunity to grow and change, but at first we are more likely to feel dejected, lost and isolated. Whilst we are depressed, not only is it impossible to see that there can be the slightest possibility of any good coming out of the situation and we will often angrily resist the idea.

Depression is a symptom, not the problem. All too often efforts to deal with the symptom are fruitless and lead to further feelings of loss, failure and pointlessness. Medication can at times be helpful in giving relief from symptoms, giving space for healing to begin, but it is only by facing and working through our difficulties that we can overcome our depression.

There are many who do not truly live, but go through life with a mild chronic depression which dulls their feelings, thereby avoiding their sadnesses, but they also never feel or even see the joys in their life. To say to anyone who is depressed that they should pull themselves together is not only cruel, it is pointless, if they could, they already would have done it.

Mostly we need someone to listen and understand us, to be with us whilst we work our way through our darkness. It is a bleak time, if someone points out a light at the end of the tunnel we are likely to believe it is a train. It is hard, if not almost impossible to believe that life will be worth living again or that we are not going to be knocked down again if we get up.

Although we may be very hard to live with at this time, however determined we are to get through this and out the other side, we will not only need our own determination but also the support of others who care.

Murder, or thoughts of

In the news we hear of murders committed by those whose partners are having an affair or have left, occasionally we hear of a special needs child being murdered by its parents. There is regular discussion about euthanasia and mercy killing. We all have our views on these subjects and how we feel about those involved, but we do not expect even the thought of such things to touch our lives.

We are not prepared for the fact that we may one day truly realise that we are capable of killing someone. This may be from intense anger and rage at someone who has hurt us, the feelings of helplessness and frustration because of constant crying or the behaviour of a child or confused adult we are caring for. Even more frighteningly the thoughts may just enter our head in what appears to be a calm and rational manner. Such thoughts are often accompanied by an enormous sense of isolation.

Though the object of our thoughts and feelings may remain untouched by all of this, we have not. It can be shattering to discover that we could do something like this, we judge how bad a person we are, how safe we are. Our whole view of ourself has changed and we question whether we can ever consider ourself to be good, kind or caring again.

This discovery is also an enormous burden, who or how can you tell anyone that you have just been considering killing your baby. What kind of a monster am I and what kind of a monster will they consider me to be. What would be the outcome, should I be locked up, the baby taken away, surely this would be the reaction of anyone I tell.

What we must realise is that our feelings are just that, feelings. We can choose whether to act on these feelings or not. To want to be rid of something or someone who is hurting us, to want to protect those we care for from suffering or a wish to do something to make things better, whatever the reasons or the feelings, is to be human. To act on these feelings would be another matter.

As these feelings are human it follows, that they are shared by many people. Because of the nature of these feelings they are rarely discussed and are dealt with in isolation, this prevents us from coming to terms with what has happened to us and in us, it also prevents us from believing that we are good or worthy.

Once we accept that we are capable of feeling and experiencing all the emotions that others feel, we can become aware of our common humanity. Just as we can understand and accept others, we can do this for ourselves and know that we can be accepted and understood by them.

Considerations of suicide

Feelings such as isolation, hopelessness and being tired of it all can lead us to feel that killing ourself is the only way left to resolve our problems.

When all that can be seen is blackness, emptiness, futility or a desperate need to get away from the pain, it is hardly surprising that suicide appears to be the only thing left to do.

It is a choice that many people have seriously considered. It is frightening to realise that this is where you are now and that you are seriously considering this possibility. The reasons other people give us for continuing with our life are rarely helpful, we have probably already considered them and this did not help. In fact it may have made things worse, looking at things as we feel they should be, as we want them to be or how others value or see them tends only to highlight our failings.

Remarks such as, you are lucky that you have your children, can make us wonder how can I be a good mother or any good for my children when I am considering killing myself and leaving them. Feeling that we are handling it all so badly, feeling and doing everything all wrong can make us consider that carrying on, is not the right answer or a relevant option.

What is needed is time to stop and to consider whether to kill ourself or not, to try and get a balanced view of the whole picture. At this stage it may be that some small thing will make us reconsider and decide to give life a bit more of a try. We may decide to finish something we started, live for the children or just decide to put it off for now. However small, this is the first and most important building block, having found this we can find the rest.

To really live we must choose to live. As we work through our grief, change and grow, life changes with us. We realise that we do not have to see the light at the end of the tunnel, all we have to do is believe it is there. Then we can begin to realise that the light is where we are now, that although things are perhaps not the way we wanted or planned, the life that we have has value and is worth living.

Blame, forgiveness and letting go

It is very important to realise that forgiveness is something we do for ourselves, it is to make us feel better and to give us the emotional space and peace to get on with out lives. Forgiveness is not only in relation to other people, sometimes we need to forgive ourselves and this can be even more difficult.

Forgiveness is about letting go of blame and anger. We do not have to let go of our memory or awareness of what has happened, we will always have these memories and feelings but these will become ones that we can live with. It is unlikely that the sadness and regret will leave us totally but these hurts will become the scars of a life lived.

When something bad happens, we look for a reason, to find out whose fault it is and who is to blame. This may or may not be reasonable. It may be that it is usefully directed into looking at what happened, either by our selves or by demanding an official enquiry to prevent it happening again or it may be that a scapegoat is needed to make everyone feel better.

Very often people hang on to blaming, insisting that there is no way they are going to forgive believing that by doing this they are punishing those they believe have done wrong, to forgive will somehow let them off the hook. What is in fact happening is the opposite, by insisting that we will not forgive, we continue to punish ourselves by not letting ourselves off the hook.

Those we seek to punish are affected very little whether we forgive them or not, they are generally unaware or do not care about our thoughts and efforts. For example, ex-partners who have left for a life with someone else, do not need our forgiveness to enjoy what they now have. A doctor that we believe was wrong but who believes he was right, may feel sorry for us, but is going to continue his life and practice regardless of what we feel about him.

We hang on to our hate, anger and blame, disabling ourselves, thinking that if he or she had done or not done whatever, then our lives would have been perfect. We tell ourselves or we believe that, if we do pick ourselves up and get on with our lives (and even worse, succeed) then the offender will feel vindicated, and we will have proved that what they did was alright or does not matter any more. Who are we punishing? Whose life is being ruined?

The hardest person of all to forgive is ourself. The blame and punishment we lay on ourselves can be enormous. We often do not even need an excuse, believing that we just must be to blame, perhaps because there is no other candidate. Here we are not only coping with what has happened but also the inability to forgive.

To forgive someone we must first feel or believe they are to blame, if we do not then there is nothing to forgive them for. If we do feel that they are to blame then we must look at what has happened, our anger and hurt and the individual's role in this. It is only when we know what we are forgiving someone for, we are able to forgive and let go.

Making excuses such as saying that someone did their best when we know or believed that they did not, or denying that we feel angry will not help. We have often been brought up to believe that hating someone or feeling angry at them is wrong, we may even somewhere feel that we will be punished for feeling this way.

Seeing others who are bitter and angry may make us feel that there is no way that we are going to be like that, so instead of confronting and dealing with our bad feelings, we deny that we have them. We may also feel that it is not for us, but for a higher authority to forgive. It is necessary that all these things are looked at, faced honestly and dealt with, to enable us to forgive and move on.

To forgive is very difficult, it can be painful and takes time, but as those who have truly forgiven know, forgiving and letting go gives peace and freedom to our lives. We may be sad about what happened and have regrets that it did, but we will know that we still have a life and that we are now free to live it.

PART 2

SOME OF THE CAUSES AND THEIR EFFECTS

These things happen to other people,
that is,
until they happen to us.

CHAPTER 1

A SIGNIFICANT LEARNING DISABILITY

Parents of children with special needs are not wonderful people,
they are ordinary people being wonderful.

Having a disabled child in the family has an effect on just about everything, such as the size of the family, whether we are able to continue to work or not, friends we would not have met, family relationships and our views and attitudes to life.

To say that having a handicapped child in a family makes the family handicapped, is perhaps too much of a sweeping statement, although I feel it is very often true. I do however feel that it creates a different family, more different than any of us realise most of the time, different to other families and different to the family that would have been.

The beginning

This probably takes place in a different time and way for each person and the actual beginning may be different from our own knowledge or awareness of it. For example, my own son has Down's Syndrome, this means that he has always been so, from the very beginning when he was conceived. I later learned that medical staff realised this when he was born, but I believed that I had a 'normal' baby until I was told differently when he was two months old.

One thing that has an effect on how we deal with having a baby with special needs, is the how and why of the pregnancy. Although two people were involved in this pregnancy, I will talk about them as individuals, not only because one may not remain involved, but also each person will have their own feelings and ways of coping. These can help or hinder, but as soon as we assume that we understand how another feels, or that they are feeling the same as us, each other, or anything, then we are creating problems for both them and ourselves.

Often the assumption is made that these things bring people closer together, the fact is that although this may happen there is as much chance that the opposite is true. A good strong relationship, with the support of family and friends will survive, but any cracks will show up and become worse if not mended.

One big problem is the way that different people deal with their grief, some need to talk others want to be left alone to cope. It is very difficult for these two opposites to work together and help one another. The person needing to talk often feels that the other does not care or is rejecting them, the one needing space feels crowded and cannot cope with all this talk and emotion. It is very important that an understanding is reached and ways of coping with themselves and each other are found.

Feelings about the baby and acceptance of it are affected by such matters as whether the pregnancy was planned or unplanned, wanted or not wanted, part of a loving union or less committed relationship. Whatever the relationship, the effect of a baby with special needs adds another dimension. A longed for baby may be deemed even more precious or considered an unwarranted punishment and totally rejected. To a larger family this baby may represent too much of a burden or a welcome addition with plenty of hands to help. As the result of a casual relationship the baby may be seen as a punishment.

There are a number of conditions that can be detected during pregnancy. If this happens the parents have to make an unbearably difficult choice, to have the baby or to have the pregnancy terminated. Everyone will have their views on what should be done, will have judged the parent's ability to cope and decided who should have a say in the decision, the opportunities for rifts and difficulties are boundless. Mostly people are aware that this is a very lonely decision that only the parents can make and are relieved that it is not up to them.

To have a condition diagnosed gives a choice, but rarely an answer, but that is what the parents are being asked to give. The decision to be made is, they must try to find the answer that is most right for them, very few will be able to give an answer that is totally right for them. It is very important that as much information and all the available facts are considered before any decision is made, but whatever choice is made, it is going to have a profound effect on all involved as they cope with the grief of their loss, whatever they decide.

There are many conditions that are not diagnosed at this time, for most of them there is no test, also, occasionally the test shows a wrong result. Some parents choose not to have tests carried out for a number of reasons, such as, because they could not consider terminating the pregnancy, because they want the baby regardless of any problems or they would not want to make a decision if the tests showed there were problems.

Assuming all is well, the pregnancy proceeds and plans are made. Names are considered, in some cases schools are booked, will I return to work, will I employ a child-minder, we need a bigger house or less happily, what am I going to do, do I keep the baby? We wonder what it will be like, will it be pretty, enjoy football, become a dustman or a pop star. Happily or unhappily we await the arrival of the baby, getting to know it more each day.

Baby is born

When a baby is born, it might be quite simple and straightforward (though that may not be how it is felt by the mother at the time!) on time, no problems. It may be that there are problems and difficulties, which need extra help but, whichever way it is, it does not mean that there will or will not be problems in the future.

The diagnosis of a significant learning disability may be made straight away, but this is not always what happens, very often the recognition that there is a problem is not made for some time. This can be months or even years later, when it is obvious that the child is not keeping pace with other children. The are also times when a baby is born perfect, but it has an illness or an accident that results in a learning disability.

The diagnosis may be definite, something that the parents can see for themselves or it may be unseen. The problem may show up on tests such as routine blood tests or it may be that because of what has happened, such as the baby arriving very early, there is a possibility of future problems, and all that can be done is to wait and see.

Whenever it is that you find that your baby has a disability, the effect is shattering. Each situation has its own special problems. Being told at the start can have the advantage of knowing from the start, therefore not beginning a relationship with a baby that you believe is 'normal' only to have to deal with letting go of this and starting again later.

Others may find that being told at this stage, has made things more difficult. They may feel that they do not want to look at the baby, fearing that they will be horrified by its appearance. They may refuse to look at or hold the baby, who they have never had the opportunity to see, even for just a few moments, as just a baby. If the baby is very ill, it may be that you are unable to hold it for some time and have to face the added fear of attached machines and tubes.

Finding out later, means that you have to let go of the baby you have been getting to know and on to whom you had transferred all the plans made during pregnancy. The joyous news of the birth you sent out, has somehow got to be followed by the fact that you no longer have the baby you thought you had and that most of your previously made plans have to go.

Late diagnosis

Often there is not a problem at this very early stage, but difficulties emerge later, maybe feeding problems, sleeping problems or delayed progress. Often parents sense that all is not as it should be, or they can see that reasonable progress is not being made and take their concerns to the doctor or clinic. These may be listened to sympathetically by medical staff, who look into the problems, but all too often, it is usually the mother, who is put down as being neurotic and may even be offered treatment for 'her problems'. At other times the parent accepts the reassurances that there is no problem, what is happening is normal, they are very relieved that there is no problem, only to be let down very badly at a later stage.

Sometimes the child's difficulties are not recognised until the child goes to school and he can be seen alongside his peer group. Even at this stage, the problems that the child has may be blamed on the parent and put down to bad parenting. It is important to be aware that there are difficulties for medical and teaching personnel, there are bad and neurotic parents but even if this is the case, no-one is being helped, least of all the child if they are written off with their parents.

There are many parents who have spent a lot of time not being believed, being put down and blamed for something totally outside their control. Often their requests for help, advice and guidance have gone unheeded and they have not even been treated with basic respect. All the while the problem is continuing, the situation getting worse and relationships, between child and parent, are becoming more difficult and unworkable.

This can have a devastating effect on parents, the hurt, anger, bitterness and lack of trust, can create enormous problems in other relationships too. For example, where a parent has believed the 'experts' rather than their partner, or the lack of trust between professionals working with the child and the parents, has become such that parents are unable to consider objectively the right school or choice of action for their child. Then they may become unable to accept support or care from anyone.

Being told
Sooner or later we are hit with the shock of knowing. This may be because we have been told or because we suddenly

just know. It may be the total, sudden shock of being told, it may be when the results of tests are given, perhaps after much praying and hoping, or it may be something that has been gradually creeping into awareness but cannot be denied any longer.

After the initial shock there is a jumble of emotions, some people remember clearly every word that was spoken, everything that was said, others have little or no remembrance of what went on or what was said. Whatever the reaction, a memory of this time will remain and will have an effect on how we feel about and deal with the future.

There is probably no good way to tell a parent that their child is disabled, but there are better and worse ways. It is necessary that the person doing the telling, cares about the parents, that the parents are given time, that information is made available, that another appointment is made available, to ask the questions that crowd in as the shock recedes. The parent's feelings must be accepted, not judged, and they must not be forced into making any decisions unless it is a matter of life and death.

It is very sad that so very often the news is given in an uncaring manner, information is not available and that what is given is wrong. Parents may be rejected for reacting negatively, or it is assumed that the baby will be rejected when in fact what the parents feel is love and care. Sometimes medical or nursing staff cannot cope with their own distress, becoming impatient with the parents and even rejecting the baby, this creates confusion in the mind of the parent.

It is very important for parents to know what the diagnosis is, from this they can find out what the implications are and what they can expect. It also indicates that there are others out there, who have coped with the same thing, therefore we are not the only ones to whom this has happened. The diagnosis shows which organisation you now can be a member of, where you will find others who have been through the same, faced the same problems and are able to give help, advice and support.

It is very difficult for parents to come to terms with something that has not got a name, this usually also means that no-one knows why it has happened and what the future holds. It is also much more difficult for parents to accept that it was not their fault, and whether there was something that should or should not have been done. It is more difficult to know what to tell others, how to explain what has happened or find help and support from others in the same situation.

Reactions

There are two things to react to, one is the loss, the other is the child. These are what will inform what happens and our feelings about it for a long, long time, often the rest of our lives.

Initially the loss is of the child that we thought we had, the 'normal' child who was to do all the things children do and the things that we had planned or thought for them. The loss is also that of being the parent of a 'normal' child and all that it means to us. Waiting at the school gate with the other parents, watching football practice or ballet lessons, the excitement of their first date, their wedding day and the arrival of our grandchildren.

We wonder why has this happened to us. We may seek comfort through believing that somehow we are special or chosen, there will frequently be others who will tell us that this is so. We may believe that this is a punishment for some past sin or a cross to bear to make us more worthy. We may be able to accept that what has happened is an accident of nature. Often we spend time searching for and reading books and journals, to try to find reasons and to help us understand what has happened, why and what we can do to make it better.

From our shocked state we attempt to look ahead. There are those who cannot cope with a vision of life with the child in it; others will see their own life totally surrounding and inextricably linked with that of their child; some will need an immediate life plan for their child, including what will happen to their child after their own death.

Whatever their view or their feelings at this time, there is a strong likelihood that these will change as the shock recedes and reality creeps in, these may well change a number of times as parents work through their grief. It may be that each parent's views, feelings and needs are similar to each other, and they are able to share their grief and support one another.

Very often understanding is not shared and the needs of each are very different, this often causes great problems. One mother may want to keep her baby and the father does not, perhaps believing that if they become fond of it they will only be hurt more later on; whilst another mother may not want to keep the baby because she feels she cannot cope, but the father wants to take it home.

Time and help are necessary to enable the parents to explore and understand their own feelings and understand the feelings of the other. Information must be provided about what the facts are both now and for the future. Unless a way forward is found that both parents are able to cope with, something of their relationship is also lost, if not the relationship itself.

Telling others

This starts from the time you find out that you have a child with disabilities. Not only is it how do you tell but also who do you tell. To say that everyone has to be told by yourself or someone else sounds obvious, but notices of a death are placed in a newspaper and this is how many people are informed. They can read about it and have time to absorb the news and decide what they are going to do.

Sometimes, when the diagnosis is made straight away, close family and friends have to be told immediately, this is shattering news for the grandparents, who now have to cope with their loss. Decisions have to be made about when and how to tell others who are waiting to hear the 'good' news. For others, the 'good' news has already been spread, now it has to be followed with the 'its not as good as we first thought' news.

Whilst dealing with their own battered emotions, the parents and family have to tell others what has happened, explain what this means and continue to be up-beat to cope with their own and the others emotions. Very often the response from others is that it is awful or a total tragedy, unable to cope with this or wanting to point out that they love this child, the parents try to modify this view a little. All too often this causes a complete change in attitude, platitudes are given such as 'you can cope because you are special', and help and support disappears.

Many people can tell their close relatives secure in the knowledge of their love, care and support. Many parents tell how wonderful their families were at this time and from then on. There are many others whose stories are not good, they receive little or no help from their families and are expected to be grateful for this. The insistence that there was never anything like this in our family, is told to many a daughter or son-in-law, firmly pushing any question of blame on to them. There are those relatives who feel or act as though this has happened to them and often attach themselves to any sympathy or praise that is being given.

Telling people can seem endless and parents wonder if each person who peers into the pram should be informed. If you are likely ever to see and speak to them again, the best answer is probably yes, because it will be more difficult the next time, or the next and so on, it also avoids that person saying something that they will feel embarrassed about when they find out. Even a complete stranger is likely to be upset or embarrassed when they are told, generally not knowing how to react or what to say. It is then generally down to the parent to make the other feel all right.

Often, to cope with this, the parent learns the acceptable facade for a parent with such a child. The bright smile and comments which say that he is loving and loved by all, chat about his progress and all is fine, reassures the other person that it is really alright and there is no great problem. This facade saves the parent from the embarrassment of crying and upsetting people. As time goes on it may well be used more and more, until very few people see or are allowed to see the real feelings.

Sometimes a parent will develop a facade so firmly, before they have worked through their grief, that they themselves cannot see and feel the pain. It is very difficult then, for them to get in touch with their real feelings and deal with them. Where any real feelings are hidden away, it is likely to make expression of other feelings difficult and relationships with others suffer. Or the feelings are expressed in ways that may be unhelpful or even destructive to the parent, such as being angry with anyone who tries to help.

Early effects on the family

When a new baby enters a family, it changes the nature of the family. If the child has a disability it changes the nature of the family not only in a much more profound way, but also in all areas of life. Initially we have our own imagined view of what the diagnosis means and how it will affect us, from whatever knowledge and information we have, to this is added what we are told by medical personnel, friends and family.

We also carry out our own search for books, journals, societies and other people to give us more information. Sometimes we are able to gain a lot of information, at other times there is very little, it may be very confusing or contradictory and sometimes we are just not ready yet to take it all on board.

If we do not have a diagnosis, it is very difficult to get any information about our child and our situation now, or find out what the future holds. This can cause a lot of distress, cuts parents off from a lot of support, it can make them very isolated and feel that they are the only ones in the world with this problem. If we do not have a name for the problem it is likely that no one has a clear understanding of it or what if anything should be done. It also makes telling others a lot more difficult as we are not dealing with facts, but trying to explain to another person something that we do not understand ourselves that has no apparent cause or reason.

Having a disabled child has a profound effect on the relationship between the parents. There are many things that may happen, there may be a number of changes in their relationship in a short space of time, as each comes to terms with what has happened and how this has affected them as individuals and in their relationship. There are numerous possibilities and each person will deal or be able to deal with them differently.

Sometimes in the time immediately after they have been told, parents become very close to each other. Their feelings for each other are intensified by grief, but as real life takes over, this level of closeness cannot be sustained so they then have to face the loss of this intensity in their relationship, as they face what has happened.

Some of the more difficult problems are; where one wants to talk about it and the other does not; where one blames the other for what has happened; where it means that the mother has to give up her plan to go back to work to care for the baby and resents this; where the mother is at home all day facing the reality and father stays away for longer and longer, working later more often, meeting with friends after work or accepting more work away from home.

These things are very often the foundations for the broken relationships that all too often follow over the next few years, if difficulties and feelings are not talked through, understood and dealt with by those concerned. How they are resolved is not just a matter of giving answers or even a change in behaviour, very often all that is needed is that each understands the other and balance is restored to the relationship.

The mother who resents not being able to return to work, given the choice, may well accept that this is the best thing for her child and choose to stay at home with them. To feel all right, she must be able to make a choice, also she must have her needs met, such as, being able to go out, to use her brain and to meet people. The sacrifices she has made must be appreciated, at the very least by her partner.

Another question that often needs to be addressed early on is whether or not to have more children, although, this decision may be changed later. The two main questions are, will any other children I have be normal and can I cope with another. The answer to the first depends on the cause of the disability, whether it is genetic or not, if it is, genetic counselling is available and should be sought, for other diagnoses, where there is no apparent cause, it may be more difficult to tell.

Whatever the answer, no honest person can give guarantees, only odds, but parents can then make a decision knowing whether or not they are willing to take the level of risk given.

The next stage

The next stage is to try and get on with a life, we want and need to do this. Somehow we have got through the early days, some feeling supported and some feeling isolated. We have dealt with a few hurdles and beginning to be aware again of what is going on around us. There are those who will be organised and moving rapidly forward whilst others are barely managing to come out of shock.

Some parents will have decided that they cannot keep their baby, they now have to make a life without it and cope with the double loss of the baby they wanted and the baby they were unable to care for. They have had to make the decision of whether and how much to remain in its life, knowing that this life will be going on without them. Their loss is great and their burden difficult to carry whilst they deal with their grief.

Some will have to deal with the death of this baby, coping with the shock of two losses. There is such great unfairness in having to come to terms with a child with disabilities, and then to lose it completely. For many, the disability is lost as the medical problems make the disability seem insignificant, the only thing that matters is the life of the child. Many hours may be spent watching his brave fight and fighting with him, willing him to live, only to lose. Such a brief life can give love and inspiration, to be carried with us through our lives.

Others will be at home with their babies trying to juggle life, no new baby leaves very much time and space, but this one will leave even less. Whilst trying to work through their grief, there is all the normal things that have to be done for a baby, as well as dealing with problems such as difficult feeding, hours of screaming or trying to put life into floppy muscles. There will be hospital, doctor, physiotherapist and other appointments, exercises to do with the baby and, if there are other children in the family, they have to be coped with too.

For siblings this can be a very confusing time, perhaps joy at the new baby has suddenly turned to grief, all attention is on the baby and everyone keeps crying. No one is paying attention to them and even if they do it is probably somewhat distracted. A very young child may feel unhappy and lost, it is therefore important that someone gives some time and attention, or at least keeps some routine going. An older child needs an age appropriate explanation and to be included as much as possible in the care of the new brother or sister, who will play such an important role in their life.

As so many appointments are in the day time and most fathers work, it is usually the mother who attends these, this can leave the father feeling outside and not part of any treatment plan or even a large part of what is going on in their family. The mother may feel resentful that she has to deal with all the appointments and make too many of the decisions, it can also be very daunting dealing with professionals, sometimes a group of them at once.

There is a lot of tiredness from all the changes, from the mental and emotional strain caused by the particular difficulties as well as those that are to be expected with the birth of a baby. This can put further strain on the relationship and the distance between the parents can grow.

Some doctors and health visitors give the mother a lot of support, others are never seen unless requested, once the statutory visits are completed.

Although most parents are willing to do whatever is required to help their child, it often seems that the parent's life and time is of little significance. Appointments are handed out, exercises given and they are reminded to not ignore the needs of their husband and other children. So much seems to be expected from the parents by themselves and by others. They are told they are marvellous and wonderful, but all too often all that is given is praise and admiration, help is not forthcoming. All too often they expect too much of themselves forgetting they are allowed to be human.

Some parents are not supported by their partner, some are not supported by their families and some do not have many friends. As at all such times, we learn who our friends are and we have usually to mourn the loss of some that we thought were better friends than they turned out to be.

Even with good all round support, there are times of fear, uncertainty and isolation. So much is expected or required; there may also be enormous feelings of loss, doubt that we are feeling towards our baby the way we should as well as feelings of inadequacy. Others may be filled with anxiety about their child, they may be full of an enormous love and protectiveness for their child and equally enormous fear that something bad is going to happen to them.

First separations

The first steps away from home, for most children, start with nursery school or playgroup and this is usually so for those with special needs. How easy it is finding a place, having your child accepted and whether it was what you want, varies from place to place and the amount and sort of provision available. It may be in mainstream or a special school and the acceptability of what is offered has to be judged by the individual parents, what may be acceptable to one may not be acceptable to another.

Many parents have already had many battles with various authorities by this early stage, and are already feeling angry and bitter towards those in 'power'. Some authorities have schemes which work together with parents offering help, guidance and support, whilst showing them how to help their child now and gradually looking at what is available and suitable for the next step. This can make dealing with the next stage when it comes very much easier.

For most parents and children, starting at nursery and school, is a big step, the first big move on the long road to independence. Someone else has total care for a part of the day and the ability to influence your child. He now has a small part of life that is not yours. He is also going to make friends, begin to develop a social life and do the things that children do.

For a child with a significant learning disability, things are somewhat different. If he goes to a mainstream nursery, playgroup or school, he may not be universally welcomed. For example, some of the other parents may not want him with their children or some of the teachers may not feel confident that this is the right place or that they can cope with him and meet his needs.

It is immensely difficult to leave him in the care of others, when his needs are so much greater; when she has a lot less understanding of what is going on; when it feels as though there has not been sufficient explanation and reassurance; when there is fear that they will not understand him or watch her carefully enough to keep her safe.

In this situation, possibly for the first time, he can be seen alongside his peers. Suddenly his differences cannot be avoided or denied. Even if they have been totally admitted to, seeing him like this can be very painful.

Although we do not know what the future holds and we remain optimistic and positive, we know that for our children this is not quite the same road as the others, that this one is likely to be longer and harder and lacking in true independence at the end. Parents are also reminded that this is also their road and that their freedom is linked with their child's independence.

He should also have a small part of life that is his own, not his parents, but chances are that his parents will hear about every little thing he has done, few actions however normal will not be linked to his disability and he will have difficulty in being himself. It is natural for parents to want to know everything and for teachers and carers to share everything, but perhaps the need is for edited highlights only and help to tell only those things which a child would wish to tell his parents.

It is at this point that many parents face a battle for their child to have a place in a mainstream school, he may or may not in the beginning need extra help. Many children will come to school well prepared and at an early stage be able to cope. For some parents seeing the progress their child has made, reading the reports of the achievements of other children with similar problems, they feel that if sufficient effort is made, their child will have the same success.

For a few this may be true, but for others there is a slow and painful dawning of the extent of their child's difficulties and a gradual acceptance, not necessarily without a fight, of what it means for the future of both their child and themselves.

There are those children who did not appear to have any problems until it was necessary for them to keep up with their peers. Sometimes the parents have been telling doctors and others that there are problems, but have not been listened to or believed. They are now expected to suddenly accept that their child has disabilities and adapt to the idea that they require special education and fit in with whatever plans are put forward.

Parents who are able to place their special needs child in mainstream education may find seeing their child along side others initially very distressing; parents placing their children in special schools or nurseries may find it even more painful; often looking at the other children in the school and thinking "mine is not like that". Admitting that this is perhaps the right place for their child to be, is very painful and for some parents impossible for a long time.

The first time of entering a school for children with severe and profound learning disabilities can be shattering for anyone, parents of a child with disabilities feel the same. Some may be able to accept this school for their child fairly easily, others are very sad to look at what it all means for their child to be here. Some parents find it very difficult for a number of reason, such as the fact that they tried to get their child into another school and failed, or because they are shocked at what they see.

They may find the children and young people in the school frightening and threatening, both in their looks and actions, they may be disgusted by their appearance and horrified by their friendliness. It is almost impossible for a parent to be able to admit that this is how they feel, they are usually disgusted with themselves and often want to just pick up their child and run away.

Usually, if a parent has admitted that they felt like this, it is in retrospect, a long time later when their child is happy and settled in the school and the parent has had the opportunity to get to know the other pupils as the people they really are. Very often by the time they are able to admit this, they have accepted much about themselves and their child and have a good relationship with the school and are happy for their child to be there. The parent often finds it hard to remember how they saw it then, but they remember how they felt at the horror of realising, though maybe not admitting, that these are like mine and that this must be how others people see him.

Whatever the nursery, then the school, the special needs child will usually be separate from his mainstream peers in a number of ways. Often he is transported to school by taxi, the school may well not be the local one so that he is not in the same school as his neighbours and he may be in a special school. Keeping contact with those in his neighbourhood becomes more and more difficult, this is compounded by the gap that grows in ability, interests and the amount of independence that is possible.

Perhaps the saddest part for many, is the inability of the child to make friends and relationships that carry on outside the nursery, or school and the development of an independent social life. For a while parents can organise this for their children in the way that any parent might, but gradually as the differences become more clear, other children go out and about to meet to be with and to do things with their chosen friends. With our children, parents have to take their children out and about, often doing activities that the parents have chosen, often with those who are the same, who hopefully are their friends.

Services and support

The care, support and services available at any time and in any area are variable, also the needs of each child and his parents are different. Some people manage with very little help, particularly in the early stages. This can be for a number of reasons, perhaps parents feel that they should manage on their own, maybe they have sufficient help from family and friends, maybe they are not aware of the services available, often services are not available or suitable. Some parents find it very difficult to ask for help because they are afraid of authority figures or of being rejected or do not want to be thought of as being too demanding. Some parents may even feel that they are undeserving of help.

It is often difficult for those providing a service to understand and accept that they are not automatically or universally seen or accepted as nice, kind and caring. Not all parents of children with disabilities are ideal, neither are all those who work in this field. Some parents have had very bad experiences with professionals they have been allocated and some parents have been very misunderstood.

There are parents and professionals who would require a saint to work with them and there are times when personalities clash. Some people are skilled at working with children but not with parents and vice versa. Some parents create difficulties because they are having great difficulty coming to terms with their problems, this may show in many ways, some are angry, some have unrealistic expectations of their child, other people or services, some look for the magic thing which is going to make everything alright.

The problem of saying this, is, that it is all too easy for parents and children to be pigeon holed, or labelled as 'difficult' or 'un-cooperative' by workers or agencies. For difficulties to be put down to parent's emotional problems rather than to face or sort out the real problems and difficulties that are present. The majority of parents caring for children with special needs cope amazingly well, they are faced with many difficulties, including lack of support and care, insufficient money, space and time. Their requests are generally modest and they are mostly grateful for any help or support they receive.

Having a child with special needs, can happen to anyone. If the child is born to excellent parents, the parents will continue to be excellent, if the parents are inadequate or abusing they will continue in this way. There are parents who will demand and fight for what they see as the rights of their children and themselves, there are those who will accept whatever they are given and never complain. Many people tread a fairly middle line, speaking up when they feel it is in the best interests of their child or their family, try to work with teachers and other professionals and to appreciate what is being done.

All too often parents requests are ignored or turned down as unnecessary, unaffordable or unsuitable and their opinions ignored or rejected. It is hardly surprising then that parents have to become angry and demanding and, at times, unpleasant. There are many parents who are mild, quiet and undemanding when their special needs children are born, a surprisingly short time later they are very different. Although wishing for a quiet, ordinary life, they have laid this aside to push, fight or do whatever it takes to get what their child or others need.

Parents generally demand most from themselves, keeping appointments, working with professionals and other parents, doing the exercises with their child, monitoring them, stimulating and encouraging them. Most do whatever they can for their child, at the same time meet the needs of their other children and partner, support others and their child's school, as well as running a home etc. Many do not know how to find the time and space to care for themselves.

All too often services are aimed at the child, lip service may be paid to the needs of parents and carers but this is all. It is a very short-sighted view, in many instances, a little support and help for carers would reduce or even remove the need for many services for the child.

For example, a parent needs respite for a few hours but this is not available, the only care available is for overnight, so a more expensive service is used because the authority cannot afford the cheaper one. Or, after school and holiday care is not provided for a teenager who cannot be left alone, to allow the single parent to return to work, so the parent has to remain on benefits, which are much more expensive to provide.

What frequently appears to be forgotten, is that the parents are the authority on their child, they are the ones who spend most time with it, this is their life and this is what they have to live. For any worker, however dedicated – this is your job, you have a life elsewhere (or should have), you can walk away from it if you want, you are choosing to be here, doing this.

There are also many dedicated and caring people who work with the children and their parents and families. They often have the problem that they are working within a system, have limited time, money and facilities to offer, they also are answerable to their own bosses. It is a great pity that they allow this to come between them and their clients, what they have to remember is the most important thing, they care.

When the future looks bleak, when services are not available when required, many parents have been kept afloat by the fact that someone cared about them and their child, that someone tried to understand, and that someone recognised their difficulties.

Friends and family

It should never be assumed that someone is receiving help and support from family and friends or that early support or promises of support will continue in the long term. For many this may be so, but for others there is very little help. Many parents are also facing the break-up of their marriage at this time, this is often an even harder loss to deal with, than discovering that your child has disabilities.

Some marriages do not break down completely, but have a frequently absent father who spends a lot of time at work, on the golf course or down the pub, refusing to admit to, face, or deal with the problems at home. Often parents find it difficult to talk to each other, to say what they really think and feel and are therefore unable to openly reach out to each other. Each may feel that the other is blaming them or does not understand what they are having to cope with, unless they are able to communicate with each other the chances of understanding and therefore helping and supporting each other is slight.

Those who may have been happy to look after a baby for a while, may be less willing to care for a small toddler and even less happy to cope with a toddler aged seven. Even where there is a willingness, sometimes individuals cannot cope. Grandparents get more frail and start to need caring for themselves. Caring for elderly parents can cause difficulties for anyone, but can be an enormous burden for someone already caring for a child with special needs.

Siblings often give enormous amounts of help and support, watching out for their brother or sister when someone should be watching out for them. Playing with and teaching their sibling, protecting them and often giving up their place as youngest child in the family to one who is learning more slowly. Gradually these children grow up and have to be given the freedom to have a life, to come and go and eventually leave home. Parents then lose not only this source of help, but have extra time to fill and activities to provide.

It is often very difficult to fit together everyone's needs and need for attention. Things have to be suddenly cancelled if the special needs child is ill, which tends to happen quite often, outings have to fit the least able if there is any chance of a tolerable time to be had. It is not easy to find time and space to give undivided attention to sibling's homework and school projects, to give support to their school and impossible to give them all that their brother or sister gets. Parents are left with many regrets and sadness, not only for the things their other children missed, but also for all the things that they, the parents missed doing with them.

Parent's own brothers and sisters can be a great source of help and support, but all too often this is not so. The good intentions are often there, but they have their own life and families to cope with. Like most friends, they are not aware of the difficulties facing the parents of a child with special needs and the grinding down effect it has. All too often promises of help are made and not kept, making the parent feel even worse or if some help is given, it will be remembered by the giver and cover all lapses for a long time.

It is very hard for parents to be grateful all the time, being grateful is a strain, so much so that not having help can be easier. Parents are very appreciative of any help provided but it is hard being reminded of the help that has been given, particularly if the help caused more disruption than the assistance it gave. This is often the reason that parents do not appear to be keen to avail themselves of help that is offered.

There is help that is freely and willingly given, by those who help because that is what they want to do (or try to make us believe that this is the case). Very often these people fit the activity to suit the child and the help to fit the parent, they are willing to truly do whatever will be of help. Such people do not over stretch themselves, so parents do not have to feel guilty for over burdening them.

They are honest so they can be trusted, if they say it is OK it is OK. Such people are the gems in our life, their light shining from their depth, helping us to find some light in ours. Unlike others who require from us the polishing of praise, gratitude and attention, taking back more than was given, their light living off ours.

Parents' groups and other parents can be of immense help and support, they are the ones who understand much of what we are going through, the problems we face and how hard it is. It is also important to realise that every parent also has their own experiences and attitudes, these may make their situation very different from our own. One child may be fit and physically healthy another ill and requiring many serious operations, one family may be rich, the parents happily married and they are in the midst of a very supportive family, the other may be poor, single and hundreds of miles away from any family.

Where there is a lot of difference, it may be very difficult for people to understand each other and to be supportive. For example, it is easy to think that it is easier for them to cope as they have a lot of money, or a lot of support, or to fail to understand why they are so miserable when we believe that they have less problems than us, but such judgements are usually made without the knowledge and understanding of other difficulties that they are perhaps facing.

Groups can also provide information, social gatherings and outings, but some groups do not like anyone to be different, those who do not feel like or agree with what the others are saying may be made to feel very uncomfortable. It may be that the group is about being up-beat, that our children are wonderful and enhancing our lives. As this is unlikely to be totally true, the group will discourage those with problems or difficulties sharing them, making them feel isolated or failures, often believing they are the only ones not coping.

It is important that you find a group that suits, helps and supports you, that you can feel part of and that you can also give something to.

Growing up
As time goes on our children grow and change, we too need to grow and change with them. Looking forward can be very difficult and painful, our child will always need the help of others and we will not always be there to provide it. We also deserve a life, but, it is questionable whether there will be a life after children for us. We wonder if the care they need will

be provided, will they be kept safe, will they be able to have opportunities to continue to develop their potential, can we remain as a part of their life but also be able to have a life for ourselves.

For some parents it is very hard to see their child as the age that they are, although they have grown physically, in other ways our children are much younger. Most teenagers with a learning disability function at a number of different levels, such as being physically mature, emotionally young and intellectually lacking understanding. They may want a car, a girlfriend, to have a job and get married but in fact may enjoy playing as equals with little children, be unable to cross the road or make a cup of tea.

We are left with a dilemma. It is perhaps easier to insist that they are not really the age they are because they are emotionally younger and allow an extended childhood, but sooner or later, they will have to leave school and we have to face the reality of the situation.

For some, the level of their ability is such that they will have to remain totally dependent. There are others who would have been able to achieve much more and would have more nearly fulfilled their potential, if all those involved had kept the person of the child in the forefront of their mind, rather than their disability. If they could have said 'lets see what he can do,' rather than 'its rather difficult for him'.

Because this child is different, contact with the 'normal' pattern is often lost. Such as, for various reasons some parents keep their children with them at all times, not letting them go, feeling guilty if they allow the child to stay away from home in any form of respite care. They worry that someone else will not care properly, whether the child will be happy, they feel that they are rejecting the child or that this is what other will think.

The 'normal' pattern is that children spend time away from home, with family friends, camping with groups such as cubs or scouts or having a sleep over with school friends. The child grows and learns from these experiences, parents begin to let go and everyone benefits from the break from each other.

As all young people grow up they have to begin to take responsibility for themselves and for others. They need to learn to be helpful, starting with small tasks at home and in school to gradually doing work, either paid or voluntary, hopefully leading to more permanent work on leaving school. Special needs children all too often are cared for, they are frequently denied a right to play their part.

This is so for many reasons, it can be time consuming and difficult to arrange for them to do this, it is easier to do it for them. It is very hard for parents to sit back and watch their child struggle with a task, they may either feel guilty for not helping, cannot contain their own frustration or it may be embarrassing. The job will be less well done by the child than by themselves, or more mess is made which has to be cleaned up or no-one has told the parent that this is what they need to do to help the child. Other people also have their need to help and feel good, this is most fulfilled by helping others, not by allowing and helping others to help themselves.

We are still having to tell the people we meet that our child has disabilities, usually to explain our actions and to save the other person embarrassment. For example, the look or comment that indicates that we or our child are thought somewhat pathetic, when we say we have to be back home for him, although he is 17 years old, turns into total embarrassment when we explain that he has a learning disability.

It is generally far easier to explain as far as necessary at the very beginning, to save any awkwardness later, but we have now possibly defined ourselves in the eyes of the other, or guaranteed the main topic of conversation, yet again.

Looking back

Many parents of children with a learning disability, have not completed the grieving process, by the time their children are much older, sometimes even after they have left school. They may be stuck at any stage, for example, there are parents who are stuck at a stage of disbelief and are having to face reality at the same time as their child is leaving school.

They have yet to face the fact that there is not going to be the happy ending that they had been waiting for, this situation is forever, the miracle is not going to happen. Some have not completed the process because they could not face the pain of the reality; some did not have the time and the space; some needed help and were not given it; for others it became inseparable from other grief from which they are suffering and it just became part of one big hurt.

For these people there is still so much pain, they look back with distress, anger and bitterness. So often they feel that their whole life has been wasted and may even feel that their child with special needs is the only good thing in it. Often there had been problems in their marriage and it has ended in divorce. To be let down by someone who you thought loved you can be far worse than having a special needs child. To be left to cope alone, maybe also with other children, creates many more difficulties.

Some cope by being over-protective of their child, others by being rejecting. The anger may be aimed at the child, ex-husband, family or the authorities (these may or may not be justified). Whatever way it is expressed, even by a firm, bright smile and 'no point grumbling' attitude, there is great unhappiness. The past is mostly seen as unhappy and negative, the future can only be saved by 'finding a rich husband,' 'winning the lottery' or 'a miracle', anything less would not work and it is all really seen as hopeless, often under a veneer of brightness.

Many are still working through their grief, facing new pain as the birthdays and other events pass by, such as suddenly realising that he should have been taking his GCSE's this year. Dealing with these things and the distress that other people cause, (even unintentional hurt causes pain) parents gradually change, becoming stronger. Gradually more able to recall even at bad times, moments of warmth, feelings of success when a new skill was mastered and appreciation of little kindnesses shown, when we were feeling down.

For others, looking back we see a very uneven pattern. Everything is linked to everything else. We have wondered, what am I accepting? What is the problem? What is the cause? Is there ever total acceptance? There were times when we thought that we were OK and the problem not that bad. This often happens when the child is young, fitting in with the family, is cute, bright, cheerful and making more progress than we could have hoped for, later we often realise that we had hardly begun. We cannot accept something that we know little or nothing about, we have to know what we were dealing with and have seen enough, to have a realistic idea of what the future holds, before we are able to accept it.

Accepting where we are now, what has passed and what the future holds, does not change the past. For those who have mourned their loss and come to terms with what they have, the past will hold many sadnesses, things we would have changed and things we would have done differently. These too form part of our acceptance, allowing us to move forward, enabling us to see the good things that happened and what we have learned.

Looking forward

This takes great courage, often we can only do it a bit at a time. It is particularly difficult when we reach a cross roads, such as when it is time for them to leave school or leave home, whenever it happens or for whatever reason.

We want for our special needs children, the same as we want for any others, freedom, independence, a job, friends and marriage. On the one hand, we are distressed that there is so much of this that they cannot achieve or can only achieve in a very limited manner, on the other hand, the very thought that they are going to do any of these things frightens us to death.

Our fears for them are much the same as they would be for any of our children, but they are so much greater. We often do not trust their ability to cope and others to cope with them, because of their vulnerability we do not feel that they are safe in the world. Some matters are of moral concern, we may accept their right and may be happy for them to have a partner, but we should question their right to have children.

This may bring us into collision with those who would deny parents a right in their child's decision making. These are they, who see parental input as interference, denial of the individual's rights or controlling, but their own input as facilitating and creating freedom and independence. Moral questions, such as, the right or not of individuals with a significant learning disability to have a child must be made with great care, taking into account all those who will be involved, it is too serious a matter to be decided by someone's political stance.

What about what the parents want or wanted for themselves. Having a special needs child has all too often meant giving up so much of the life they had planned and wanted for themselves. From space and time in which to do what they wanted, the freedom to consider a future for themselves, the career they were going to have and the savings and pension that would have seen them comfortably through their old age.

For so many parents, the future is a bleak place for both themselves and their children. At the present time, with many cutbacks in services, it looks as though a future where our child was cared for away from home, possible a short time ago, is no longer a possibility for many. Their child will have to stay at home and there will be little or no respite. For many parents this means that they will not be able to return to work again, committing them to the rest of their life as a Carer on benefits.

The future is not a settled place, however hard we try we cannot see what it holds. There have been many battles won and many still to fight, for both our children and ourselves. We have learned from past experience that we can cope with more than we ever though possible.

If we have worked our way through our grief, we will have left behind the anger and bitterness and will know that whatever the future holds we can cope.

CHAPTER 2

ADULTERY

They absorb the guilt and suffer the pain,
in isolation, to protect the guilty.
All too often the innocent are blamed,
for what someone else has done

Some attitudes and beliefs

The way adultery is dealt with in such things as the media and on film, the way it is often seen and talked about and the myths and attitudes that are generally accepted, all tend to ignore the pain and suffering that it causes.

Usually the focus is on the affair, there is great interest, curiosity and entertainment. Even if we do not approve, there is a certain amount of vicarious pleasure in disapprovingly hearing about it. When the rich and famous are involved, newspapers are sold in their thousands and it is a favourite topic of conversation, how dreadful, wicked, stupid, how could they when they have such a gorgeous partner or whatever are acceptable comments made, but rarely is it simply described as wrong.

There are attitudes and beliefs such as; monogamy is not natural, therefore affairs are bound to happen; men are unable to remain faithful; men do it so why not women; so many people are having affairs which just goes to show that it is more natural than not, therefore you should expect it and not be surprised when it happens. Beliefs abound that it is good for a marriage; that it adds spice; that many marriages are better after than they were before; affairs meet natural needs that are not met within the marriage, thereby keeping the marriages stable.

Everyone has a view, everyone knows what those involved should have done and should do now, whether they are famous or the people next door. The messages are mixed and confused but are usually put forward with great conviction and rarely take into account the wider picture.

It is interesting that the one who is considered the wronged party, the one who has been hurt and is suffering, is the one who many feel should 'do something' or take control and 'deal with it' whilst trying to cope with themselves and the situation. They are also often considered to be the one to blame.

They are thought to be at fault because they did not make enough effort, were not caring enough or were being boring. We might ask, how does having an affair with someone else really appear to be a good way to remedy this. Consideration that perhaps working something out together or ending the relationship if it is intolerable, enabling you to be free, might be more constructive are rarely commented upon.

It is often stated that after having a baby, the tired, probably sore new mum with very unstable hormones, whilst anxiously trying to cope with the enormity of caring for a new baby and keeping the ordinary things of everyday life going, must make sure her husband is not neglected or feels left out. Such articles and comments just add to the pressure for the new mum and presumably give a lot of men an excuse for remaining immature, not taking responsibility for themselves and their actions and blaming others for their faults.

Many men must find such articles and comments very insulting when they are considerate of their partners, share in the care of their child and do not need their partner to define or make their place in their own family.

When affairs happen, partners are often told not to be weak, not to show distress, hold your head up, do not have them back. If you are weak and have them back you are only giving them permission to do it again and they will probably end up leaving you.

Looking at this it seems that, though it may or may not make a difference to the adulterer, at the end of the day the innocent one has lost, whatever they do. It is quite likely also that very few people have much choice in how they react, we react as who and what we are, the reaction to being hurt is usually more of a knee jerk reaction than a planned one. We can however be left feeling much worse because we believe that we did it all wrong.

When we have been bereaved, particularly where there has not been a death, we are very likely to be judged and criticised by anyone and everyone (in public, if we are famous enough) for the way we respond to and deal with our bereavement.

The choices are impossible, either to stay with an adulterer and maybe something can be worked out, or give up my marriage, probably my home, my standard of living and cope with everything alone. This would also mean a split up of the children's home, but we are unable tell them the reason for this as it would probably upset them and damage their relationship with the other parent. We all accept that a child would not be able to understand what has happened and why, but this is also true of most partners and many other people.

There is still a double standard that says, even if it is not OK for a man to commit adultery, it is still considered worse when committed by a woman. It is hardly surprising that society finds it hard to say unequivocally that adultery is wrong and those involved are responsible for their actions and the consequences, when so many people have affairs and it is common amongst those we would wish to look up to.

Living a lie

Both the person who is having an affair and their partner are living a lie whilst one of them is having an affair, the difference is, that the person who is having the affair knows this, their partner doesn't. It is obvious then that they are both living different lives. The partner who is having an affair has to lie to their partner and probably to the person with whom they are having the affair, perhaps about their marital state or the state of their marriage. They also often lie to themselves to have an acceptable reason for continuing with their deceit.

In this situation, so much of their life is built upon deceit. One knows this and the other does not, but even the one who does, lives with the knowledge that if they were found out, they do not know what the outcome will be. Any plans for the future are built on very shaky ground and it is questionable that the person who is ignorant of what is going on, would make the same decisions and plans if they knew the truth.

For example, many women become pregnant whilst their partners are having affairs, they may well want this, but would this be so if they knew what was going on. Their decision is made in the belief that they have a faithful partner and their relationship is secure.

Whilst there is an ongoing lie, there cannot be true and open communication. The one partner will always have to be on guard, making sure that they do not let anything slip, mention a place they had been, or saying 'we' when there should only have been an 'I'. Such things make for gaps in conversation, guards are put up and conversation discouraged as it is tiring and difficult. The other sensing the tension, feeling the difficulty and becoming concerned often starts to try and find out what the problem is.

Feeling insecure, they may keep on asking what is wrong, questioning their love or fussing in other ways, this concern is often interpreted as nagging and can even be turned into the excuse for the affair happening in the first place.

Often there is an insistence that nothing is wrong or it is blamed on stress and long hours at work, this can make the innocent party believe that what they have to do is try harder, take over more of the chores or leave their partner alone, often denying their own needs for the perceived good of the other. If this goes on for too long, or becomes the norm in the relationship, it can lead to further complications such as resentment. Guilt at having an affair can make the person angry and bad tempered at home, making life very difficult for all, if this can be used to blame the family, there is further excuse for not being there.

There are many who say that the time spent with their lover is so much better than time spent with their partner or more relaxing or whatever. This is like saying that being on holiday is more relaxing than being at work, the responsibilities have been left behind, but particularly where there are children, one is left behind to do the work whilst the other is away 'on holiday'.

There is a tendency for there to be a mixture of old and new attitudes which can be used to fit whatever scenario. Such as, we are supposed to be able to work, play, have children, run a home and still look good, also we are expected to be happy and fulfilled, it is OK to grab at happiness – everyone else does.

Any of these can be taken to justify whatever we do, the opportunity to have an affair can be put under the heading of a right to enjoy oneself, "I am stuck at home all day looking after the kids, I deserve..." or "I go out to work, come home and help, I earn the money, they spend it, I deserve..."

We are told by other people and magazine articles that if we become dependant we will drive them into the arms of another and if we become too independent they will not feel needed and will go to one who needs them. If we become a doormat we will be walked on and if we become assertive they will be frightened away. Caring new man is a turn-off and macho man is for turning off.

These are all excuses enabling people to avoid facing up to the fact that there are no real excuses, relationships need openness, honesty and fidelity. It is for each person to be responsible for their own actions, admit their own part and be aware of the consequences of the choices they have made. Others need to be aware that this is not some sort of game but for real, as is the pain, the damage and the loss.

Before knowing

It is often said that you know when your partner is having an affair and that if you don't, you are just not admitting it to yourself. This is sometimes true, at other times you are aware that there is something wrong but believe that whatever is wrong it is being caused by something else. There are also times when there is no awareness that this is happening, particularly in the early days, before evidence to the contrary has built up.

There are those who are untroubled if their partner has an affair, or believe that they would be. This is their choice and something that they are able to do, but it should not be held up as the only way to be. This attitude can make those who are devastated by their partner's affair, feel that they are an even greater failure, because they somehow believe they should feel, act or respond differently.

Sometimes the discovery that your partner is having an affair comes totally out of the blue, sometimes a picture unfolds more slowly. We might be feeling that life is OK, much the same as ever – but – well, its a bit funny that a pair of jeans were packed to wear during a formal conference, or boxer shorts are suddenly worth a try, the lift from the friend was met down the road not at the house as usual. At first such incidents are hardly noticed, then they linger for a moment needing us to explain them away to ourselves, to remove them from our mind.

Then maybe a trace of doubt begins to linger, so perhaps a carefully framed, casual question, is the next step, as we begin to fail to convince ourselves that all is well. We perhaps wonder, half aloud why the clothes smelled different as they were put in the wash, we may receive an equally casual reply, perhaps about the testers on the perfume/aftershave counter, you may even feel guilty when told that you have just spoiled your birthday surprise. Are they having an affair or am I just being silly or putting our relationship at risk myself, by doubting it?

Talking to friends often is not of any help, they each come to the discussion with their own views about such matters, depending on their attitude to men or women, relationships and their own experience. They may also attempt to protect us by keeping us in, or getting us out of the relationship, regardless of what the truth might be, often their advice is about how they feel that we will be best protected, rather than about what is right for us. There are many friends who would not tell us even if they knew that our partner was having an affair, to tell or not tell puts a friend in the very awkward position of not knowing whether they are going to be believed or rejected.

Families do not necessarily support and protect their own, they may be helpful and supportive, listening and trying to understand, helping you to work out the best way forward, but often they will be unsympathetic, blaming you for ever having doubts about your partner. This may be because they cannot tolerate the idea of a marriage break-up, or because they like and care for your partner, if they face up to the possibility that there is an affair happening, they will have to re-think their relationship with your partner and face their own loss. Sometimes to stop you questioning the situation, they may even suggest that if it is happening it is probably your fault.

There are those for whom this time of unknowing is filled with flowers, presents and surprises, the guilt is dealt with by giving extra time and attention. For others their partner is increasingly irritable and bad tempered, there is no way in which they can be pleased, each little thing that is done can be a source of friction, there is nothing in the home or the relationship that may not be a source of criticism. The former may give rise to doubts about the motives of the partner, the latter tends to give rise to doubts about yourself.

Many people have lived through this anxious and unhappy time when there are no problems but they have difficulty in trusting their partner. For many others their initial sense of unease and their growing doubts cannot be settled, if they ask they are likely to be told that nothing is going on, the doubts persist but are the doubts in me or in the real world?

We bring to such a situation our own attitudes and prejudices, how we feel about those who had affairs, how we feel about their partners, what we think they should do, how we believe it all should be.

Finding out

Whether we suspected anything or not, the shock, confusion and sense of revulsion are often staggering. The very thought of it may make you throw up. The anger can be so great that you want to attack and hurt someone, the sense of hurt and betrayal so overwhelming that all that can be done is to collapse into a heap, feeling so much of your insides have been taken away it is impossible to get up again.

In the confusion of jumbled thoughts and feelings, there is a desperation to know everything, who, where, when, how long, but at the same time we do not want to know anything. To hear is to beat ourselves up, but at the same time hoping that we will hear the something that will make it feel better, or make sense of it, or enable us to understand why.

The other person probably wants to off-load and tell you everything, to hand this all over, to make it someone else's problem, but at the same time wanting to say nothing. They may be realising for the first time what they have done, they probably did not mean this to happen and are having great difficulty dealing with the reality of what they have done. They are therefore not coping well and are probably unlikely to do anything that will help in the slightest and are likely to do everything very badly.

Very few people are able to understand, consider or believe that the affair is about the people who had the affair, they are the ones that had the choices and made the decisions, even though they often insist that it just happened.

The partner did not have a choice and they have been dropped into this, but they are very likely to take much of the blame and guilt onto their own shoulders. The self-doubts generally do not creep in, they hit you, what's wrong with me? where did I go wrong? what should I have done differently?

All this hits at the very core of a person, the way they look, the shape of their body, the way they dress, walk, cook, talk, have sex, run the house, treat the kids, treat their partner.

It is often felt that the affair is proof that they are not good enough, their total being has been rejected. Some people are able to get angry, they are aware that at least they have some value, and their life and efforts some worth. Others feel that this has proved their lack of worth, their total lack of attractiveness and their inability ever to have a relationship or be treated well and valued.

There is an enormous loss of self esteem, feelings of stupidity, all the clues are remembered, "how could I not have seen?" "why didn't I realise?" A lot is suddenly explained, we realise why certain things happened, why things had felt all wrong at times. The past is gone over time and again, we ask ourselves many questions such as, "what could I have done differently?" "why didn't I demand an answer sooner?" all the time, looking for what we did wrong and blaming ourselves.

Feeling angry with ourselves we remember the blame, we put on ourselves when we had doubts about our partner. We may remember how self-righteous they were, when they said that the problems were because of us and the way we were. We should be able to feel self righteous now that we know we were right and they were wrong, the problem was them not us, but it does not matter anymore, it has all gone and we have all lost.

What about the third person in this, we may well think of them as bad or evil, generally we need to feel that either they or our partner are the one who is to blame for this situation. The feelings of anger and hatred towards one or both of them are enormous. We often cannot face the full fact that they chose to do this, to do what they did, to hurt us so much, we may need to place one of them, often our partner, in the role of helpless victim.

It can take a very long time before there is even the slightest chance of us being fair, reasonable or able to look at the situation with any objectivity.

What was the reality?

If we discover that this affair has been going on for a while, we have to face the fact that we were not living the life that we thought we were. Many doubts and fears surface as we look back and wonder when or if ever our life was the way we thought. Where is the solid ground? Is there any truth anywhere? Can anything they say be trusted? The sense of betrayal is even worse if the other person is known to us, had been a guest in our home, shared our food and we had considered them to be our friend. Who can we trust anymore?

We may want to be hugged, reassured, comforted by our partner, but how can they, because at the same time the thought of it may make us sick. Anything said, any reassurances are hollow and empty, we do not know where the truth is any more, we have made fools of ourselves by believing them, we have been hurt by trusting. Our judgement of the honesty and reliability of the person closest to us was wrong, how can we ever trust, even our own judgement again.

We need to be held, but in those arms where another so recently was? The love, the affection, the sex were supposed to be special, for just us, but where is the specialness now. It has been shared with others without our knowledge and agreement, was it ever special? It is now lost forever and we often feel stupid for believing it. The thought of them together brings pain and revulsion and often appears repeatedly and at any time, like a flashback in post-traumatic stress disorder.

Some may be able to accept their partner having a sexual relationship with another person, the hurt is caused when, whatever they believed was special and only between the two of them, has been shared with or given to another without their knowledge or consent.

It is hard to cope with such facts as; whilst you were at work or coping at home with the chores and the children, whilst you had taken on most of what there was to be done, perhaps to help them as they were very busy, they were having fun with another, sharing what was supposed to be special to you both and not caring that they had left all caring and responsibility to you.

This can give an overwhelming sense of loss and aloneness, the one person who should be in this with you, helping, sharing and caring with and for you, the one who should be there to care and build a life with you has just given it all away and has become the one who has created for you, this pain and loss.

This is especially so if you have also been left with the legacy of a sexually transmitted disease. For some, this is actually the way that they discovered the infidelity. When being treated for an infection, they were asked about other partners they have had. This is totally humiliating, knowing that they have been faithful, knowing that they may not be believed and realising that their partner has not only been unfaithful, but has also given them a disease, with all the risks it carries and the humiliation that goes with it.

We may be aware, or it may gradually dawn on us that other people may know about the affair, that they may have known for a long time, they have been watching, maybe pitying, maybe blaming. Who are they? Who can I ever face again? How can I face the embarrassment and humiliation? We see ourselves in their eyes, as we saw others in ours, we and they judge as we know people in this situation are judged and as we judged others.

What is there to do?

Very often, the decisions and responsibilities for what to do next, are suddenly, all in the hands of the one who has been hurt. Often within hours of finding out that this has been happening, at a time when it is impossible to make a proper decision, they are being demanded. Decisions such as, do you want them to stay or leave, what do you want them to do, what are you going to do, are you going to tell any one and can you ever forgive.

Under pressure, some decisions are made. For some the important thing will be to save as much as possible from the wreckage of their relationship, others will feel that anything other than getting rid of it in an attempt to rid themselves of some of the pain would be impossible, yet others wish to hide it away in secrecy feeling that the pain of others knowing and judging would be too much.

The consequences of any actions at this stage are unknown but you are aware that if anything is said to anyone, so many others people could be hurt, this includes, not only immediate family, but extended family, friends and possibly your career. It is a heavy responsibility and we wonder if we must carry this alone. There is also an awareness that any decisions made now will be hard to undo or change.

Most of us believe that we know what we would do if this happened to us, well away from reality, we may decide that we would not stand for it and they would be out. The reality rarely looks like we expected it to and usually the response is very different to the one that we expected to make. What is at stake is often a joint home, joint children and a difficult to manage on, joint income. Whether to lose all this is now our decision, we have done nothing wrong, nothing to ask for this and none of it is of our choosing, but this is what we must do. We must care where others didn't, be responsible where others weren't at a time when we have been severely hurt. It is a very cruel place to be.

All too often the consequences are that this is suffered in silence, with no support or care, no-one to talk to, probably no-one else even knows that this has happened or at least that we have found out and are suffering. When we were young, optimistic, strong and happy, we knew that we would not stand for this, does this mean that we have dropped so far and are now old, defeated, weak and sad.

Having off-loaded, the relieved partner often takes on a new lease of life. They thought that they had thrown everything away but have been given a reprieve, the initial feelings of guilt and remorse fade as they then move on, often becoming increasingly impatient with a partner who is taking time to recover.

As no one has let them down, they have not lost trust and faith in others, they have until now remained in control of the situation. Now they are not in control and it can be very frustrating, making them feel guilty or impatient to get life back to normal. There is often surprise expressed when someone who has had an affair is shattered when their partner has one, somehow it is expected that causing hurt feels the same as being hurt.

Telling anyone else is very difficult, once someone has been told there is no guarantee that they will not tell others, it is again difficult to know who knows. There are many people who may well judge you, particularly those who believe that this has happened because there is something wrong with you, or in some way you must be at least partially to blame.

If you stay together you will be considered weak and stupid, anyone you talk to now will always know and it will always be there, whatever I tell them can never be forgotten and for how long will the often unasked question, "is everything alright?" be hanging there.

Deciding to stay

Is this the right thing to do? Who can say. At present this is either what you want, or what you can cope with for now. There are many doubts that you will ever be able to get over this, trust your partner or other people again and be able to let it go. You wonder when will things ever return to normal again and be the same as they were.

The important thing to realise is that neither you, your partner or life can ever be the same again. You are embarking on a new relationship, a new way of life and being. Like anything new it has to be learned, it is therefore uncomfortable and strange for a while. So much that was taken for granted has gone and we cannot just be in the relationship any more. The doubts and fears that keep rising, have to be calmed, reassured and dealt with, sometimes alone, sometimes together. Emotions are unsteady and everything in life and everything that happens, seems to be a reminder of what has happened and where we are.

For many it is a time of information gathering from any and every source, in an effort to understand why it happened, what to do now and to realise that you are not alone. The subject it seems is there, on everyone's lips, on every news programme, in every magazine, newspaper and book. This may be to some extent reassuring, but there is also no escape from the subject. It may be open day for many famous people, and many couples who have split up, but there is still an enormous cloak of secrecy not only hiding those who are attempting to keep their relationship afloat, but keeping them in isolation.

It is strange to think, that in any place where there are a lot of other people, you are probably surrounded by others suffering the same, others who have been through it and others to whom it will happen. Sadly each moves on in their isolation, we do not know who they are, they do not know of us and neither of us know how to make contact with each other to give contact and support.

As with any bereavement, it fills every part of your thoughts and life, whilst at the same time you are trying to get on with your life, but here, you are also trying to act as though nothing has happened. Because no one knows, they also carry on as normal, often dropping casual comments about others and their affairs, which can make you feel as though you have just been kicked.

Others will make complimentary comments about your partner, such as, how good and kind they are, or how lucky you are to have such a good relationship, the control needed, to cope with this can be enormous. The children sensing or probably hearing that there are problems, keep up a barrage of questions, some of which it is impossible to answer honestly, such as are you going to split up?

Often there are grave doubts that it will ever work, but if there is complete willingness, commitment, honesty and determination to make it, then there is a chance. There are those who say that it made their relationship better, usually this is because they did not realise what they had until they nearly lost it. Having gained a reprieve they decided to work at it together, to communicate and do whatever it takes to make their relationship work.

Many other people get stuck in the grieving process, unable to get to the point of forgiveness of either the other or themselves, or fins they are unable to begin to take the first difficult steps towards rebuilding trust. Others try to carry on as normal, trying to ignore what has happened. Some believe that because it is something that happens so often, they should just be able to accept it and get on, others believe they will lose more if they make a fuss, or do not believe that they have sufficient worth to expect anything better.

To move forward together, both have to grieve for what they have lost. Lessons must be learned from the past, enabling new and better communication, intimacy and understanding to develop.

Deciding to split

For many, to stay with an adulterous partner is impossible, even so it is very hard to have to be the one to end the relationship. It is a decision that may well have a question mark over it, however small, for the rest of your life, should I have given them another chance? Was I somehow to blame? Did I make the right decision? Could I have done something else?

Everyone will now want to know why you have split, do you tell them? We are often strangely embarrassed that our partner has had an affair. There will be much discussion with us and without us about the rights and wrongs, where the blame lies and who has suffered.

Decisions have to be made, what to tell the children, the parents, other family and friends. Should everyone be told the same story, do you tell them together or apart, and so on. Everything has to be split and all the things involved in a break-up have to be negotiated.

Very often, although it may be your decision to part, your partner does not want this. They are very sorry for what they have done and want you to be back together, to give it another try. They may try everything they can to find a way of reconciling the situation. This makes it very difficult to cope with the conflicting emotions of longing for the partner and relationship you had and the hatred for what they have done and who they now are.

It is very difficult to know what to tell children, it is bad enough to have to tell them that you have decided to split and are consequently hurting them, but do you tell them why. To tell a child that one of their parents has had an affair, causes them great problems, not only shattering their view of their family, but also of the honesty and integrity of that parent.

They have to look at the time that they considered theirs, that the parent spent with this other person and the fact that this other person was considered more important than them or the rest of the family. If the child does not know, is honesty being compromised and if they find out later, will this cause them further problems.

There may be sympathy from others who know the situation. There will also be pressure both subtle and not so subtle to get you to change your mind and to re-think your decision at the same time as you are getting told that you did the right thing. All this is very confusing, maintaining any sort of emotional balance can feel almost impossible. The grief and sense of loss and loneliness are enormous.

Some rush into another relationship, if this is done before the lessons are understood and learned they will fail again, all too often being attracted to someone very similar to the one who was left, only to end up causing ourselves more grief by re-enacting the same story. Others find that it is almost impossible to trust anyone again so they avoid making new relationships, in the hope of not being hurt again.

What we need is time to grieve, time to learn, time to grow and support whilst we do this, then to have the courage to trust, so that we can find love again.

CHAPTER 3

DESERTION

When someone we love dies, they had no choice in leaving us.
They leave us their love to carry in our heart and help us in our grief.
When someone we love leaves us, they had a choice.
They leave us their rejection to carry in our heart,
the cause of our grief.

Looking at break-up

The breaking up of any relationship is painful, even one that was short and unsatisfactory for both the people involved. Coping with rejection hurts but, it is also difficult being the one who is doing the breaking-up.

Even when we are the one who is ending the relationship because we were not happy and it is what we want, it is very rare, not to feel at least a little bit bad about hurting the other person. It is difficult to know how to tell them, there is no nice, easy or kind way to do it, just some ways are better than others.

Where the relationship was longer and deeper it is even more difficult. More of ourselves, our time and effort have been invested in it, there are more things to split up, leave behind, or take with us. We are leaving behind both the good things and the bad things that have happened. We now have to adapt to a life without this relationship, even if this person is still in your life, this particular relationship has ended.

To lose the one we love is painful, to come to terms with regrets, anger and resentment is very difficult. It is not very often that we can walk away from a relationship without having a number of feelings to deal with, we may also have to deal with the feelings or results of the feelings of the other person, friends and family. Sometimes the one who has been left will not let it go, perhaps believing that the relationship can be resuscitated, even when we know that this can never be so.

We may even be positively euphoric that we are out of this relationship at last, but the relationship did happen and we have spent some portion of our lives, however small with them. Rarely can this be walked away from without a backward glance. We question ourselves about the time spent with this person, what of the time we feel we have wasted, what of the things we did, what of the things we did not do, and where did the early happiness and optimism go. We question our motives, our choices and feelings and wonder how we could ever, possibly have liked them, done what we did or even fancied them in the first place.

This is a time of adjustment filled with doubts and fears. We realise that we have changed and that we are a somewhat different person to the one who was in the relationship, also different to the person we were before. Through all our relationships we learn, grow and change to some degree.

Not only have we changed within ourselves, many things in our lives have changed. We may have moved, changed job, had children or many other things may have happened such as a parent dying. Some of these things will be because of the relationship or part of it, other things will happen just as part of life moving on. When the relationship ends we realise that we cannot go back to where we were before, that is a life that does not exist any more, it also has gone. Much of what has happened during the life of this relationship, will remain in our memory, connected to it, such as the fact that we got this job whilst we were going out with Jo. There may also be regrets, such as, realising that we should have spent more time with a parent who has died, instead of the person who has now gone.

The break-up of any relationship, like any change can be painful and difficult but it can also be very positive and a time of growth. This depends on a lot of factors including the causes, the time the people have been together and the commitments they have made.

Some relationships and endings

Many relationships end by mutual agreement, both parties realising that this is the best way forward for each of them. Often they can help each other through the break-up, remembering and talking about the good times, being aware of what has been learned and gained from it. There may be a sad ending, but they have supported each other in making plans for a new but separate beginning.

There are many reasons why relationships do not work out and come to an end, all too often it is what one person wants and not the other. Sometimes we have the problem of how to end the relationship, at other times, we are the ones who have been left and are broken hearted. When we were young, most of us had a number of boy or girl friends, with whom we had relatively short relationships, these were part of growing up and learning about ourselves, other people and what we wanted from life and future relationships.

Sometimes in long term relationships, the one who has decided to end it is the one who has made most of the effort to keep it alive and make it work. Eventually they realise that this is pointless and that they should be in a more worthwhile relationship, where the effort to make it work is shared, as are both the chores and the good times.

There are those who have been abused mentally, emotionally or physically by their partners and have decided that they cannot or are not willing to take any more. Such people have often invested a lot in this relationship and therefore have a lot to give up, to lose and leave behind. It is difficult to say 'this is it' when the voice inside is saying 'perhaps if I try a bit harder' or 'if I give it a bit longer, perhaps things will change'.

These people will feel very much the same as a person who has had been deserted, but for them there is the problem that they are the ones to make the decision to end the relationship. Knowing that they could go back, or feeling that, perhaps this time, if they went back, it would all be different and alright, makes staying away very difficult.

The difficulties involved in leaving, coping, starting a new life, with problems such as shortage of money, loss of home and coping with children, may make the past look much more rosy and the future together look positive and tempting, however wrong this view may be and however well this is known.

In such a situation the one who has been left, is also probably not too happy about it, they may well be used to having someone to control, do their cooking and cleaning for them and now life has become much more uncomfortable. They may well be working very hard to get their partner back, putting on the charm which has not been seen since courting days, bribing the children or being useful and affectionate for the first time in their lives.

It is very difficult to watch someone we care about, return time and time again, to an abusive relationship. It is hard to understand why or how they can do this, and, it is also often difficult to see what it is about the other person that attracts them. All too often whatever we have to say falls on deaf ears and there is nothing we can do or say to change things, all we can do is wait until they realise this for themselves and decide for themselves that they must leave for good.

There are those who appear to have a great partner, to anyone outside the relationship it appears to be really good and they appear to be very lucky to have such a wonderful partner. Any comments they make to the contrary are not heard, or they are considered never to be satisfied, not telling the truth or totally unaware of how lucky they are. Bruises show, at least to ourselves and should make us realise that this is a relationship we should not be in.

Mental and emotional cruelty does not show, it is a gradual process, neither those abused or those around them are really aware of what is happening. Often there is a subtle undermining of the whole being of the person, quietly destroying them from the inside. A comment here and a look there, leave a bad or unhappy feeling, but this appears to be out of all proportion to what has been said or done, so it is dismissed and another downward step has been taken.

Gradually quietly and gently, support systems and the opportunity to look clearly at what is happening have generally been eroded, so that, being ill-treated, unsupported and lacking in care, has become the norm.

Often emotions are confused, love is seen where there is none and a realistic view of what is reasonable or unreasonable is lost. It is very difficult and it often takes a long time for the person in an abusive relationship to realise this and to leave.

Before desertion

Usually before someone leaves a marriage, they have been unhappy in it for some time. They may have been planning to leave for a long time or it might be something that they suddenly decide to do. Some people leave because they do not believe that there is anything that they can do to make it better but others do not want to even try, often their wish is to be out of the relationship, perhaps to be in another. They feel that this is what they have to do, either, because they have no other choice or because there is another, preferable one. For the one who is left there is no choice.

During the time leading up to this, there may not be any signs that this is going to happen. Often partners are kept completely in the dark, if they get concerned they are reassured that all is well, or that this is just a bad patch and it will go away. Sometimes the relationship has obviously deteriorated and there have been efforts to find help to sort it out, but these will not stand any chance of being successful unless both of the people in the relationship are committed to making it work.

For many people their commitment to this relationship and to the promises that they made to themselves and each other, either publicly or privately, are taken very seriously and they will do all in their power to keep them. There are also many others who do not have this commitment they may even have decided whilst they are making it that if it becomes uncomfortable they will leave, consequently they make little or no effort. They believe that they have a right to do whatever they want and that they should not have to change anything about their lifestyle that they do not wish to.

In the time before the break-up, some people do not feel a difference in their relationship, others may have a sense of discomfort or insecurity. They may be aware that something is wrong and may try hard to make it better, this is very difficult to do if you do not know what the problem is. Often there is a gradual distancing, more time is spent apart, the other becomes gradually less involved and less caring about their partner, their children and their home.

Sometimes there are fights and shouts of abuse, for others there is the silence of no communication. For some the effort of trying to make the relationship worthwhile has been given up. They have accepted that they will stay in it for what there is, such as financial security or a comfortable home, unaware that this is not a choice as their partner has decided to leave.

During this time both are living to a different agenda. Often one is aware of what is going on both in their relationship and in the others' life, the other, unaware that they have no idea of what is going on, they carry on believing that things are as they appear or as they have been told. This may make them feel uncomfortable, but if they ask their partner about it they are likely to be wrongly reassured or rebuffed. Feeling rejected and often helpless the gap between the two widens, this is often used as the excuse for the final break-up.

Why did it end?

The full or true reason for leaving is often only known to the person who has left, there is also the possibility that even they do not really know or understand what the true reason is, or are refusing to acknowledge it even to themselves. What other people are told, may be the truth or the truth as it is seen, or just what they are supposed to believe. It is therefore very difficult for anyone else to really know what the situation is and probably unwise to make any firm decisions or judgements.

All too often people expect too much of a relationship, they believe that if they find the person of their dreams they will be happy, if they find the right person and marry them, their problems will disappear. If they are not happy, they often think it is because they are not in the right relationship, so they go out and seek for the right one.

Few people want to spend the rest of their lives alone. Those who are alone, those with broken or unhappy relationships and even those who want to be free to play the field, spend much of their lives looking for the one. The same energy is less often put into keeping it and making it good, once it is found.

Many people feel that life would be alright if only... I had a job, or a different job, or didn't have to work, if I had children, or didn't have children, if we could spend more time together, or if I had more space, if I was with someone else etc. All these may be true, we might be fine and happier, if things were different, but so often it is more a matter of the grass on the other side of the fence being greener and we fail to see the potential happiness in what we have got.

It is not just one thing that makes our life or relationship good, so it is unlikely that changing one thing will make it right, if there is general dissatisfaction. Where there is only one problem, it is often possible to deal with and change this without getting rid of everything. All too often a relationship is thrown away because another situation appears to offer the thing that is wanted, only later to discover, that in fact, the sum total of what was thrown away was bigger than the individual item, the importance of which had grown out of all proportion.

Some people want to leave because the relationship has become boring, others want to be free, they may want to escape the ties and responsibilities that have been collected or to start afresh with someone new. Whatever the reason, very often the decision to go is unilateral, giving their partner no choice.

Leaving

To be told that your partner is leaving and that all the things you had together are gone, can be to feel that the bottom has dropped out of your world. At some stage in the future, you might look back and decide that it was the best thing that could have happened to you, but at this time, it is more like the end of the world.

The break may or may not be expected, but when it happens it is an enormous shock. Some people are told as their partner leaves, some people are not told at all, their partners just disappear leaving them to believe that they have been killed or injured, leaving them to search, wait and hope. There are those who tell their partners that they are leaving and then stay until the right time or right accommodation is found, expecting them to cope with living apart, together.

You have just been told that your love, care and all that you have to give, are no longer required. There is a better life for them, without you in it. Because they have decided that this is right for them, you have to give up your way of life, maybe your home, standard of living, manage on your own, give up the children or cope with them and their unhappiness on your own. The person you love has not died, they have walked away from you, but the legacy they have left is very similar.

You may not be wanted, but you continue to want to be wanted, you may not be loved anymore but you continue to love and care. We try to believe it is a mistake, they will change their minds, or there is just something that they or us do not understand or realise and soon it will become clear and we can return to normal. If there is not another person involved, we believe that given a little space and time that they will realise that they have made a mistake and come back. Even if there is someone else, we may believe that they will realise that we were better, change their minds and return to us.

This state of disbelief can continue for a long time particularly if it is encouraged by our partner or by others who want to see us back together or are helping us to believe what we want to believe. It is also encouraged by the fact that there are those who do get back together again.

The habit of caring and the love we feel usually does not just stop, very often we continue, for a while, to care for and protect the one who has left us. We will not hear bad things said about them, we intervene to prevent the children saying the angry things that they want to, we worry that they may not be managing without us and often check up to make sure they are coping.

This behaviour may appear strange to others but, as with any bereavement, the lost object is searched for, their place is kept in readiness for their return and for a while, it is mainly the good things that are felt to have been lost and that are remembered.

We are suddenly in the position of having to make a lot of decisions about things we know very little about. Things that will have an enormous effect not only on our lives but on the lives of others, including our children and our families, such as, how and when to arrange access? How, and what sort of relationship do I have with my in-laws? What do we do about our future relationship and how do we cope with it? How do we know if it is best, to see them or not, if so how often? What contact should the children have?

It is impossible to know what the future is going to be like, what will be needed and what the effect of the decisions we make now will be. We are having to deal with all this, whilst coping with the double pull of the feelings of love and longing against those of anger and hatred. The problems continue, questions such as those about contact in the future, do not have a straight answer, they depend on so many things. Also, what we feel and want now may be very different to what we will feel and want in the future.

Very often, the right decision is not the one we want or need. For example, it may be best for the children to continue to have contact with both parents and for the parents to at least be civil to one another but it is very difficult to cope with this when seeing the partner again causes so much distress and anger. What we want is never to see them again.

Although they have left, hurt us badly and caused so much loss, we still have to see them, speak to them and deal with them. This is the person that you loved and committed yourself to, the person with whom you shared and built a life, a home, had children and planned the future, the person who you were going to grow old with. Now you are supposed to behave as though this can be just switched off and a new and different relationship turned on.

Each time you see them you are reminded of the way it was, what has been lost, each time they leave it is a re-enactment of the leaving and you again feel bereft. They are there, but they have gone, they look the same but feel different. In place of conversation there are arrangements to be made, agreements to come to.

We want our children to be happy, we know that it is important that they have a good relationship with both parents. But to see them getting hugs and affection that are no longer yours, to hear them happily planning treats and outings that you are no longer part of, to plan your own time alone when it should have been time for family, is very hard to cope with.

It is hard to learn the jobs that the other always did, the ones that are too heavy, too difficult or just too much when you are tired and coping alone. Many screws have been driven into the wall with the force of anger, hurt and frustration behind them, difficult to thread needles and half wired plugs thrown across the room, followed by the anguish of "I shouldn't have to be doing this".

More decisions and people to tell

Not only are you married and not wanted, you wanted to be married. To add insult to injury, you not only have make decisions about what is to be done and who has to be informed, but you also have to go around and tell people.

Family have to be told and their reactions dealt with, they may be sympathetic, helpful and supportive, but you are not the poor grieving widow or widower but part of a failed marriage. They not only have to deal with your distress, but also their own feelings of prejudice and of failure and of loss, they also have to tell their own relatives and friends that their child's marriage has failed, they then have to deal with the reactions they receive.

Although we had no choice in the matter, we still have to deal with the questions of why, when, how, will it mend and what are you going to do? Then listen to the suggestions about what we should do or should have done.

The list of people to notify about the split and the consequent decisions made seem endless. Schools – "will you please let me know if there is a problem", cubs and brownies – "yes it is fine if they make a card for fathers' and mothers' day", the bank – "can I please take my name off that account and have another" and so it goes.

On many forms there is a box requesting status, if you are married, your status has now changed, on some forms it is easy if painful to tick separated, on other forms there is the choice of single, married or divorced. You realise that none of these describes where you are, you are legally married but single, single but legally married.

If you are female, you can make decisions about what to call yourself, perhaps changing yourself to Ms.? You could return to your maiden name, but not the person as you were, she has also gone.

Coping with the break

There is so much to do, particularly if there are children involved. Their life has just been shattered and it is up to you to try and put it back together again, to give them the care and support they need, to continue to provide a stable home environment even whilst you are falling apart yourself.

It is hardly surprising that in the early days we probably manage very badly. There often seems no point in carrying on, if this is where our best efforts have got us, how can we expect anything to work out in the future, if this is how we are treated when we trust someone, how can we ever trust again. We are tired, there is so much to cope with, we want to be left alone, but if we are we do not know what to do with it and the space is filled with pain.

We think about how much better off we would be if they had died, we would have got so much more sympathy, no-one would ever have dreamed of considering that what has happened was our fault. The insurance payments would have paid off the mortgage so that we would not have had the financial worries that we are coping with now. We could have believed that they are with us in spirit, wish to be with us and do not want to be where they are, but our reality is that we often know where they are, what they are doing and with whom.

Initially we are often at the mercy of out thoughts and feelings, remembering things, realising now that things were not as they seemed, wondering how we could have been so blind, feeling that we had looked stupid, feeling angry at our weakness and helplessness. Very often alcohol is used as an anaesthetic for the pain, but it just adds more confusion to our jumbled thoughts and feelings.

For a while we stumble along, hurt and crying, feeling the unfairness of it all, feeling the lack of care and support from others, weighed down by the enormity of it all. We may find the support that we expected or hoped for from our families but this is not always the case.

Friends may stay and support us, but many will not, some will disappear immediately, some after the initial upset when they have got fed up with us not recovering quickly and others cannot cope with us recovering. There are those who will avoid us, perhaps for fear of contamination, or they do not want their children to mix with single parent families, or they are afraid that they might lose their partner to you. Some joint friends will consider that they have to choose and will go with your partner, believing that there are sides to be taken.

It is very likely, that you will feel that there are definitely sides to be taken, and yours is the only possible one. The enormity of the hurt and injustice that has been done is proof of this. It can be very hard to understand how anyone can take the other side, and it is hurtful to hear those who insist that there are two sides to every story or that you must be somehow to blame. If this comes from those who should be supporting you such as family and close friends, you feel that you have been delivered a second blow. It increases the sense of isolation and aloneness, making you realise that you have lost even more and have in fact got very little true or safe support.

We need to be told that we have value, that we were worth holding on to, that because one person did not realise or appreciate this, does not make it true. It is they who are the losers for not appreciating what they had, it is they who have lost and it does not diminish us or remove our worth in any way.

As time goes on, hopefully we gain greater insight, a clearer view and more understanding of what happened and what it was all about. We may see that there were ways in which we contributed to the break-up, these can be placed in context and learned from. On the other hand, if we see that there was nothing that we could have done that would have made any difference, we must learn what lessons we can from this.

Some feelings about the children

In the early days we spend a lot of time looking back, at first we often regret everything about the relationship, it takes some time to be able to see and accept the positive things. Other people pointing out how fortunate we are, rarely helps. There are those who tell us that we are lucky to have the children, this can make you feel guilty if you are not appreciating them at that time.

If your partner has died, the children are a part of them for you to keep and treasure, a constant reminder of your love for one another. A constant reminder of the person who has shattered your life is not quite the same thing. The children are a continual source of guilt, feeling you have let them down badly, feeling that maybe you should not have had them as this is what you have done to them. If you are in no way to blame for the break-up, this adds greatly to the sense of helplessness.

The children have to be balanced along with all the other things there are to do and all the things that there are to worry about. It is very hard to watch their suffering and unhappiness, their sense of loss, helplessness and confusion. They have lost the basic security from their lives that all children should have and are having to learn about the painful realities of life before they should have to. You may long to help, comfort and make everything all right for them, but you cannot do this. Often you cannot even get past your own distress to help them and they are the ones who end up doing the comforting and caring.

Your partner may well now be mostly free of their responsibilities having given them to you, they may have also taken your share of freedom and are free to build a new life for themselves if they wish. You have probably been left with less time, money and freedom, without the children you also would be free to make a life. Dealing with such choices is very difficult for some, but even when the choice is easier to make, it is hard to live with the consequences. It is difficult and painful to reconcile your love and care for your children and your feelings of resentment and anger towards them. There are feelings of guilt for what has been done to them, we know they deserve better, this is not what we promised them and ourselves when they were born.

We can get stuck at any part of the grieving process, some parents become and remain depend on their children, reducing the child's freedom and autonomy, the child takes over the caring role exchanging places with the parent. Many people find themselves in this situation for a short while and feel very guilty about it. The level of caring that is expected can vary from comforting a distressed parent to putting a drunk one to bed, or from doing a little babysitting with the younger children to give a short break to managing the house whilst the parent runs wild.

Many parents and children find that they develop a mutual caring and understanding whilst supporting and caring for each other. In our efforts to help our children we are helped. Whilst helping them to understand, we find understanding; before we can expect them to forgive, we must learn to forgive; if we want them to be gentle with themselves and others we must learn to be gentle with ourselves and others; if we do not want them to blame themselves for things that are not their fault we must stop blaming ourselves.

We do not want this to ruin their lives and future relationships but we will often allow it to ruin our own. What we wish for them we should wish for ourselves and then take the lead in finding it. The best way to teach is by example.

Some of the cost

Financially we are probably much worse off than we were, although if the person who has gone had kept us very short of money, perhaps because they were a spendthrift or a gambling addict, we may find that managing on our own we are better off. We may have to give up working or work for longer hours, which may cause further hardship.

Many are forced to move out of the house where they have lived, often into something smaller and less convenient. The children may be very distressed at having to leave their home, they may have to give up having their own room and have to share with brothers and sisters, leading to resentment of each other and the parents. We may have to leave all the work we have put into the house and garden and all the memories that go with it.

Some people have to leave the area where they have lived, leaving behind not only a house but also friends and a way of life. This is an enormous change for everyone and probably includes new schools for the children, a further loss to their security, an increase in their feelings of helplessness and lack of any control in their lives.

We have lost a way of life, a partner and the status and recognition that goes with it. We have probably been part of a world of couples, now many of them will not know what to do with us, a single person can be difficult to place. We have lost the ease of going out as a couple, it is hard to face things on our own. The confidence to go to parties alone is hard to find even if there are any, there seems to be no point in going on holiday alone, the fun has been lost. Christmas, a time for families, has been spoiled and may even have to be coped with alone and without children.

Splitting everything costs money and often any savings disappear or have to be shared, even when they are yours. There are also less tangible losses, such as only one person to run the kids about, no one whose place it is to baby-sit even for a little while. Even though they may never have taken any responsibility, now they have gone, we have to admit that the burden is ours.

There are many who have put a lot of love, effort and support into the relationship in the belief that they were building a future for the whole family, only to lose it all and be left back at the beginning. This is often at an age when it feels too late to begin again. So many have put all their time and energy into building up a business together or supporting a partner whilst they became educated and trained. They have cheerfully given up holidays and treats, working long hours, managing without so many things, believing that there would be benefits in the end. Unfortunately, only to find that once they have become successful, their partner has exchanged them for the one they wish to share the benefits with.

This is a very cruel thing and all too often the partner who has been supportive is left without the time or means to start again on their own account, frequently they have also lost their pension. They have consequently worked hard and given up a lot, but have not gained anything, this is worse than nothing. What they have made, someone else has taken, committing them to a very poor future and old age. It is very hard for those to whom this has happened, to get past the regret and bitterness and begin again.

Building a life

The new life is built on the old, how far we have cleared away the old and understood what went wrong, will have a lot of effect on how safe and secure our new building will be. If we have not learned from the mistakes that were made, they may well be repeated, we take things with us from the past, whether we want to or not or whether we are aware of it or not.

Whilst we are sorting out the past, our attitude towards much of it may change. For many it will not look as bad as it did and there will be positive things we can take forward. For others a clearer view will make it obvious that, what they were living through before the break, was in fact so much worse than they had ever imagined.

They may not have realised this before, because they were not aware of the way things were and what was happening to them. Having got away, they are not now living in fear, or having to be careful about how they look, what they say or what they do. They are now aware of the difference and can see the strain they had been living under. Initially the loss of strain may take some time to get used to and it may take a long time before they are able to relax and enjoy where they are now.

For many people there has been a loss of trust, caused either by their partner's behaviour, by being deserted or by other losses that they have suffered. There are a lot of people who have suffered a number of losses and being deserted is often the culmination of this. The lack of trust is not just of possible future partners, but may well be of all members of the opposite sex or, even, most other people.

Regaining trust in ourselves, our life and in other people is a very difficult task, partly because it is very difficult and painful to learn that this is something that we will not be right about all the time, that there are no guarantees we will not be hurt again. As we build our life we learn new coping strategies, we learn not to have such thin skins, we become better at knowing who to trust and who not to. As we change and grow we attract new and different people into our lives, we can learn not to be a victim and to be aware that we deserve better than we have received so far.

Many of the friends we though we had will have gone from our lives, it is often difficult to tell why they did this and we are often very hurt when it happens. As we grow and change there are others who cannot cope with the changed you or do not wish to. They needed you to be the way you were and are not willing or able to change themselves to cope with your changes. Some do not want to have an equal relationship with you and needed you with your problems and difficulties to make them feel better about themselves and their lives.

Many practical matters have been sorted, from the splitting of belongings, what you are going to do with the children, to access and maintenance payments. The arrangements are very different from one couple to the next so it is very difficult to know if what you have decided is good or bad, right or reasonable. We are not very good at splitting up, even the best arrangements are just making the best of a bad job and it is as we begin to look back that we can begin to judge whether we have made a reasonable job of it or not. Some will have decided never to see this partner again, others may never negotiate anything directly but instead enhance their solicitors life-style, yet others are able to work together towards having a reasonable relationship and giving the children the best that they jointly can, apart.

All building takes time, it has to be done properly or it will not last. We need to make sure, as far as is reasonably possible that we do not put things into the life we are building that are unsound, do not fit or we are aware they will at some time in the future crumble. We are now able to see and make choices, such as knowing that we do not have to take ill treatment from others and that there is often more than one way forward. As we move through the grieving process, we are able to regain our balance, look up and move towards the future.

Divorce and after

A divorce is the legal ending of a marriage. What we also have to do is find the way to mentally and emotionally end the relationship and move forward with or without the person in our life. How we feel about this may well change as time goes by, but particularly where there are children from the relationship, it will never completely go.

Having become single again, we may be wanting to get into another relationship or we may know that there is much to be learned before we do this, if only, how to make a better choice next time. There are others who have decided that they will remain single as this is the way they wish to be or because they are not willing to put themselves in a position where they can be hurt again.

Some people are able to see life in a positive way, (it may have taken a lot of time, effort and grief to achieve this) they set about building a life of their own, realising now that they are important and do not need a partner to give them worth. They can gain strength from this belief, but this can only be gained if the true work of grieving has been accomplished.

There are many who achieve much, driven by their anger or despair, but they have not resolved their feelings which remain as raw as they were when they were deserted. There are also many who remain bitter or who feel that life is unfair and owes them for the pain they have suffered. This prevents a sound base being prepared on which to build and more hurt will follow, either to themselves or to others, such as when someone whose partner has gone, feels justified in taking the partner of someone else.

There are those who strive to achieve, but driven by their anger or their need to fill their lives to avoid thinking about what has happened to them or to feel the pain that it has caused. Avoiding their feelings means that they also cannot feel the joy and sense of achievement that comes from their efforts.

Some people refuse to let go of their anger, feeling that if they continue to have a miserable life, somehow it will make the other person suffer. Some feel that they have to be in a relationship at all costs, they feel that they cannot survive alone and often again choose badly. For others, the break-up gives them the opportunity to make a new life, have a new and better relationship and to feel that they have learned and grown from the experience.

We need to take time to work through our grief, understand ourselves and move on, we need to re-think our life and our values, we need to care for and support our children, whilst they work through their grief at their enormous loss. It is a tall order and a very uphill struggle, the way is very unclear and we have to make our own path. There are many slips and slides but we learn that the aim is not to reach the summit as fast as we can but to enjoy the journey, for that is what life is.

CHAPTER 4

A RELATIVE WITH ALZHEIMER'S DISEASE

Gradually we watch the one we love leave us,
to become a dependant stranger we cannot know.

Confusion before diagnosis

In the beginning there are mood and behaviour changes, sometimes exaggerations of existing behaviour such as being more fussy, forgetful, anxious, questioning or irritated about things. This is often attributed to what is happening in their life, the changes or pressures in personal or work life that they are coping with. This is particularly so if they are relatively young.

Life becomes more confusing and difficult for them, feeling fearful, they often try to cope by covering it up and excluding others. We cannot know what is going on, but often feel confused and frightened as we feel them becoming distant from us, we then think up our own explanations, often making life even more difficult for ourselves. The distancing makes us aware that they are leaving us. We fear that this is something that they are choosing to do but are not telling us about, we do not know or understand that this is something that they have no control over and that they need us with them more than ever.

No one knows what is happening, often even the doctors do not know. There may be many attempts at diagnosis and treatment, often the problem is believed to be caused by depression and they are then treated for this. It is difficult to know what to do or what is happening, we keep hoping for a cure or for the situation to resolve itself, but all too often the suffering and not knowing can go on for a long time.

There are many problems as they gradually get worse. They may get lost and forget things, it becomes difficult to trust them to do anything and if they are working they will eventually lose their job. Their personal care and hygiene will begin to deteriorate and it becomes embarrassing for them to be in public. Added to these, their behaviour may become bizarre, aggressive or unpredictable. It will become increasingly difficult for you or any one else to be with them for long periods of time without breaks because of their behaviour and the level of care that they require.

When the diagnosis has been made, it can come as a relief, at least we know what we are dealing with, we now know that what is happening, is not their fault and we can stop looking for a cure. It is also heartbreaking, to know that there is no cure, no reprieve and that this downhill trend will be and is for the rest of their life.

We may be filled with dread as we look forward, our fears are for both them and ourselves, as we wonder what this means, how we are going to cope and how long this will be for. We do not know what the future holds. Determined to do all we can for the one we love, we may make promises that we will be unable to keep, promise such as; we will always look after them ourselves, or in their own home for the rest of their lives.

The child as carer

Parents care for their children, they love and support their children, they are there for their children to turn to when ever they are needed – everyone knows that.

However much we know that this is not necessarily true or that our parents will not be there for us one day, it is always a shock when it happens. It is very difficult and painful to change roles and for a child to become the carer of a parent. When a parent has Alzheimer's disease, the child becomes the parent of a parent becoming a child.

We may feel very let down, angry, hurt and confused. We still need our parent as a parent, someone to lean on, talk to and always be there for us, we are not ready to give this up yet. We are even less ready for them to need us, especially in such a total way.

Those who did not have a parent who they could lean or rely on, who were not loved and cared for by their parents or had been ill treated, are now being expected to look after and care for a parent who did not do this for them. To give up part of their life for a parent who gave and gave up nothing for them, to treat well a parent who ill-treated them. They will have to face the hostility and disapproval of professionals, family and those around them, if they do not do what is required of them.

I need to think – am I willing to do this, how far am I willing to go, can I cope and how long will it be for. What are my responsibilities and what responsibility am I willing to take, what can I cope with and how will it effect the other areas of my life.

It is very difficult to admit to thinking in this way and it makes us feel very guilty, we feel that we should not be thinking like this, but should be willing to do whatever we are needed to, whatever the cost. It quickly becomes obvious that however sympathetic others are, they also generally feel that we should be willing to give up our lives if necessary.

There are many things to consider and each individual's situation is different, it makes a difference whether you are living with your parent, living nearby or far away and what sort of career you have. There are very few jobs that are able to fit in with your being a carer. You may spend regular periods of time away, or be at home every evening, you may have a big supportive family or you may be the only one willing or able to help, it may be that you have other members of your family to care for.

Your lifestyle also affects how others see you and what they expect from you. If you are single, female and live locally, it will be assumed that it is no bother for you to cope, you are probably not considered as having anything in your life, including your work and your partner, that cannot be put aside at a moments notice.

It is quite likely that you will have great difficulty in getting help and support, the expectation will be that you could always go and live with and care for your parent or they could move in with you. If you are female and married with a family, it is assumed that you can fit your life around the caring, your family will be expected to cope whilst you care for your parent.

If you are a single, professional male you would be unlikely to be expected to cope, your work is important and you would not be expected to know what to do anyway. If you are male and married, the expectation is likely to be that your wife will do the caring for you.

If you do not fulfil these expectations, there will be a lot of criticism from many people, not only those who are having to do the caring if you do not, but also from many people who are not even involved. There will be phone calls at all hours of the day or night when people are anxious about our parent, often these will be from neighbours or those who know them and feel we should be informed of what our parent is doing. It also enables them to hand over responsibility. At the slightest problem we are expected to drop everything and run.

This presents a difficult dilemma, it is very good and kind of people to be concerned and take the trouble to let us know. Part of us wants to know what they are doing, but the part of us that is not able to do anything but worry, does not. When we have done all that we can, what more can we do.

If no safer place can be found, or the parent refuses to move to that place and the authorities feel that they cannot force them to, should we give up our life, home and family to stay with them all the time? There are many people who will call us uncaring and ungrateful if we do not, but they appear to be unaware that we live in permanent fear for our parent, but to do other than what we are doing, would result in the loss of everything else in our lives, including our own health.

Some children will be willing and able to become permanent carers for their parents, they feel that this is what they want to do and dedicate themselves to caring for the parent for the rest of their lives. Many other children are not able to do this, some are not physically able to manage, others have commitments which make it impossible for them and there are others who are not willing to make any effort even though they are able.

Caring for a parent

As children we coped with our parent's moods and behaviour as a dependant. As a grown up child we may have achieved something close to equality, but whatever the relationship, it is very different to coping as a carer to a parent with Alzheimer's disease. Here, the responsibility shifts from your parent to you, we begin to feel or believe that we are responsible for things that we cannot be responsible for, causing us guilt, embarrassment and anxiety.

Caring for a parent with Alzheimer's disease, will give us many such concerns. Their behaviour can be very difficult, they may have very bad moods, accuse the neighbours of damaging their property or wander into their neighbours' homes and refuse to leave and even helping themselves to their food. They may wander out in the night, inappropriately dressed, give their belongings away or get lost. Their strange behaviour can cause much embarrassment whether this is trying to buy goods in a shop with buttons or accusing someone who helps them of stealing their money.

Coping with them will become a strain, their behaviour is likely to deteriorate and everything may become a struggle. They can protest against anything and everything creating difficulties, from getting them to eat, to getting in the car, having a bath or changing their clothes. Nothing can be done quickly and the mind is stretched finding ways to coax, cajole or even force them into doing what is necessary, what is necessary becomes what is achievable.

As they are able to do less, it is necessary to take over more. It can be very difficult, embarrassing and distressing to perform very personal tasks for a parent. If the parent is aware, even for a short while, it is even more difficult. To clean up a parent, as you would a small child, or to become in their mind their parent can make you feel confused, lost and lonely, the world has become topsy-turvy, it is very scary to realise that your security is now you.

We think of our parents as they were. It is horrible to imagine how they would feel about the way that they are now, the distress and embarrassment it would cause them. If they are sometimes still lucid, we have to cope with this distress, at their dependence or their rejection of us because of their dislike of their dependence on us.

We also look at how we feel. Our hurt and shame to see them like this, we often hate ourselves for our embarrassment, impatience, resentment and hate of them. We rarely see what we are managing but are well aware of what we are not managing, we see what we are doing badly but not what we are doing well.

They who cared for us as a child are now being cared for as a child, their dignity is gone and they are no longer our parent. Our parent gradually left us, there is not a date to mark it by, but we cannot deal with this anyway, whilst we still have to care for this deteriorating person in our parent's body.

If and when it becomes impossible to cope, somewhere has to be found for them to be cared for. It is highly unlikely that this will be somewhere that you like or they would have liked. Not very often will they want to stay and the guilt at deserting and giving up on your parent can be enormous, it is very painful, even though you may have no choice but to do this.

It is also sad that at the end of the day, brothers and sister who should be sharing in the work, the care and the problems, who should be supporting and caring for one another, all too often find that they are left with anger and resentment towards one another when their parent finally leaves them.

Caring for a partner

A partner can develop Alzheimer's disease when you are both much too young to have to face and deal with it, or when you are too old to have to cope. Just the same as it is with a parent or anyone else, it can take a long time before the condition is diagnosed. Before this, whilst the disease is developing both of you face many doubts and fears about yourself and each other. Some of these can be shared, but often many of the fears are carried alone.

Any equality in the relationship is lost as they deteriorate, you will have to take more and more responsibility, until you take full responsibility for everything, including them. It is very difficult for love to survive. Where the relationship had already lost its love, the one left to care will find it very hard to continue, feeling trapped and resentful, in a relationship that gave them nothing whilst their partner was fit and now there will be nothing given by them, but everything given by you.

For many people, their marriage vows were taken very seriously, they feel that they must carry on as they promised they would, until death parts them. There are many people for whom it is an act of duty, for others, to continue caring is an act of love. It is what they want to do for the one they love, the one who would have done the same for them for the love they shared.

It is difficult carrying all the responsibility for your home, your life and your family, it is even more difficult and painful to also take responsibility for another person who can no longer take responsibility for themselves. To add to this, is the fact that all the work, thinking, planning and caring are also down to you. Not only are there all those things that you would have had to do if they had died, but there is also all the caring for someone, who is gradually becoming more and more dependant, confused and difficult to manage, as well. Initially they may have been very brave and shown a lot of courage in their fight to cope and to carry on, but now the courage shown is yours.

There is likely to be very little help and support available, it is up to you to find what there is and to get it for yourself, even though you may not have the freedom, time and energy to do this. Family members who become carers are usually just expected to cope however difficult the problems are.

In situations where carers are paid, have off duty and holidays, where they are trained to cope with problems. If they cannot cope, they send the person home to their family carer who just has to manage, with none of the benefits or breaks.

It is very difficult to get a break or any time away, some carers receive help from members of their family, but very often this is not so, or the help that is received is very little, inappropriate or too much gratitude is expected. As time goes by, nights will become disturbed and it becomes increasingly difficult to get enough rest and sleep, enough time to do the chores or to have any life for yourself. There is an almost complete loss of freedom and the care that has to be given becomes total, just like caring for a very difficult and large, young child. They have to be washed, dressed, fed and watched all the time to keep them safe.

There is usually a drop in income in the early stages leaving very little to manage on. It is very difficult to cope with paying for everyday expenses and essential items, therefore to afford any extras to make life more bearable can be impossible.

Although they are aware it is not their partner's fault it is easy to become angry with them, feeling that their partner has let them down and left them to cope. They feel resentful that they have to care for their partner, that they have lost their freedom and that they are doing this alone. Other people feel angry at God, the professionals who they feel should be giving or providing the help they need, or their families for the lack of help and support they are receiving.

There are people who have spent most of their life caring for little or no reward. They have not only cared for and raised their children, but over many years have cared for elderly parents and often aunts and uncles through their last years and final illnesses. Now when they are old themselves and should be receiving help from others, they are facing having to care for a partner with Alzheimer's disease. Instead of at last being able to spend time alone with each other, to do the things they had wanted and planned, they are having to spend, the last part of their own active years, caring for their partner and watching their hopes, dreams and life disappear completely.

What is and what should have been

If our marriage is good, we want to have time together after the children have grown up and left home, to do all the things we could not afford and did not have time to do, we want to grow old together. If the marriage is not good, we hope that as time goes by it will change, that we will grow together and have a life that will make staying together worthwhile. We look forward to enjoying having time together to enjoy our successes, our home and the grandchildren, an easier life when there will be space to relax and do what we want.

If the marriage is bad, you may have been considering leaving and had been planning to be free once the children are independent. You may have decided to stay but to get on with your own life, reaping the benefits of the home and income you have worked for and deserve because you have stayed together.

If your partner develops Alzheimer's disease you may well feel that you are now tied together forever, the only way out is death, how can you leave now, how can you ever have the life you promised yourself and each other. To wish for your freedom is to wish for their death, initially it feels wicked to do this, but later their freedom through their death is a release for all.

It is very difficult to be caring when all your feelings are of anger, hate and the unfairness of it all. It is difficult enough to care for someone who you loved deeply, but it is particularly difficult to care for someone who did not care for you when you needed it or treated you badly. Now you are tied to them giving up your life to care for them, as they become more dependent. It seems that there will never be anyone to care for you, they did not in the past and are not able to now and there is not now the opportunity to perhaps find someone who will care.

There may be things in the past that are regretted, some perhaps could have been remedied but now there is not the opportunity or space to do anything about it. Perhaps you feel that you should have left or not even married them in the first place, but now you are tied to them, every minute of the day, coping with every need, whim and mood. You feel that you do not know how to deal with this but also you certainly do not want to learn.

Your children suffer, particularly those who live at home. They have lost a parent who should have cared for them and been there for them, they are often confused and resentful, finding it very difficult to understand what this illness means. You will now need to be the parent who is there for them, the one who comforts and supports them and tries to help them make some sense of what is happening, although you will probably not be able to do this for yourself. They on the other hand will now be expected to be good, kind and helpful and to learn to support and cope with a stressed parent who is learning to cope.

Their life is likely to become more restricted, there will be less family outings, parties and fun times for the young ones. The older ones will have less freedom as they will have to stay at home more to help. The carer parent will be less free to help in the ways that they otherwise would, to give lifts and to do all the other things together that they would have liked or been willing to do. It is very difficult to invite friends to the house, as it is embarrassing both for the children and their friends to see a parent like this. The confused parent may not be able to cope with other people around, or any noise or music, so life may become very restricting.

For the carer parent, it is difficult to know what a child's duty is, how much can they be called upon to do before it affects their study, family relationships and the relationship they have with their parents. Home may become a place to be avoided and to be got away from as quickly as possible.

This is not the sort of family and the relationships that we had planned. Even when they are good, so much of what we should have had and done together has been lost.

Trying to cope

With the diagnosis comes many feelings and many fears. We may feel relief as we at last know the name of the problem and what we are dealing with, we feel guilt for the times when we have been impatient and we have more understanding of why things happened, what is going on and what the future holds. This also brings with it fear for the future, for both them and our self.

We need to grieve for the loss of the person that was, the one we knew and loved. This is made difficult by the fact that they have not yet gone, they are still with us. Physically they will be with us until they die and this may be a long time away. Although the amount of time they are as they were, gradually gets less and more infrequent, there are moments of lucidity for a long time. If the diagnosis is made at an early stage in the illness, there may be the opportunity to talk together about what is happening, but we are also able to see their anxiety and suffering as they try to cope with and understand what is happening to them.

As they become less and less in touch with us, we wonder where they have gone, why this should be happening, how long will it go on for and whether we will survive it. Sometimes the personality remains one that is not too difficult to cope with, but all too often they become very unpleasant and difficult to manage for at least some of the time. We find it very difficult to cope with the thought of this happening to us, or other members of our family and become fearful that this will happen.

It is difficult to know how to be with them, we wonder what they know, what can they feel, are they aware that they have come to this. We wonder how we can continue to cope with someone who is so totally unaware of us and does not care about us any more. There is no response or encouragement, no caring about our pain and tiredness, no sharing in anything any more.

Fear that they will die turns into fear that they will live, the guilt of thinking and feeling this lies alongside the fear that we cannot cope much longer. So much in our life has had to be given up and our needs and wants have gradually become more simple, we ask for a night's sleep, to do the shopping unhurried or have a coffee with a friend. We begin to forget what it would be like to have the space or money for a holiday or a proper break, if we did have one, could we ever come back again to this.

To get any respite is difficult, all too often others in the family do not share in the care, this can cause splits which never heal. We question how far we are responsible, how far others and the wider society are, but mostly this is just an academic exercise which just leaves us feeling more angry, resentful and trapped.

If there is any care offered, perhaps in a day centre or even perhaps a longer break, we have to pray that they will go, that those who run the service will help us to get them there and to stay. It is very cruel to deny a carer a break because the person who is cared for would rather not take up the offer and would prefer to stay at home. This may be understandable, but the rights of the carer need to be supported and protected, if only to keep them able to continue caring.

There is also the problem of a difficult to cope with person having nowhere to go or being banned from the place they were attending. It is again understandable that they cannot continue to attend somewhere where they cannot be coped with, but this should prove that extra help is needed by the carer and lead to this being given, not the withdrawal of services so that they have nothing. It is so hard to fight for a service when you need the service because you have no fight left.

Time for the next move

When we are able to admit, or are forced to see that we cannot manage any longer, we have to look at other alternatives. The thought of having our freedom again, space in our lives to do what we want when we want to, gives rise to many mixed feelings, such as, relief, apprehension, joy and sadness. The thought of where they will be and why brings us feelings of guilt that we have let them down and sadness that it has come to this.

The places that can be considered are usually not what we want at all and we do not like to think that someone we love will have to live here. This has to be balanced by the fact that this is what there is and the concern that we may not be able to find a place for them. It is very difficult to find anywhere that we are happy with and possibly impossible to finds anywhere that they will really like and accept.

We feel guilty at our rejection and the fact that we did not cope to the end, although we know that we do not really have a choice. We also feel anxious that they will not agree to go there or agree to stay, we worry that they might be thrown out because the staff cannot cope. There is in fact, every chance that they will behave better when they are not with us and are being cared for by other people.

Once they have settled in and their affairs have been attended to, there is still the visiting to be coped with. This may be the time when we still feel that we are able to do our bit, even though they may not even be aware of our visits, or it may be a nightmare that leaves us anguished and drained.

However much we are aware that it is not sensible we often still want to make a connection with them, to clear up unfinished business, for them to say what we want to hear, or for them to understand that we have things that we want to say.

Having got them as settled as possible, feeling totally drained from many years of caring we now need to make a new life for our-self. It may be difficult to know where to begin and there is still the final goodbye to be said. There will be a need to grieve for the life that has been lost and the life that has been had, both theirs and ours. We may now wonder, after all the caring that we have done, who will care for us, now when we hardly have the strength or will to start again or later when we are old and frail.

We grieved for what we ourselves have lost and for the loss of the one we loved as they gradually left us. It is not until we are finally released by their death that we can see their life. Their death frees them from this life and enables us to be free to live ours.

CHAPTER 5

A CHILD'S HOMOSEXUALITY DISCOVERED

Just to be who they are, they face losing those they love.
Those they love must lose the one they thought they were,
to gain the one they love.

Some expectations

Just as we do not expect our child to have disabilities, we do not expect our child to be homosexual. To many people the whole idea would be totally alien and unthinkable. As the child grows up they become aware of their parent's wishes and expectations for the person they are supposed to be and the life they are supposed to lead.

Often parents are not very aware of the expectations that they have of their children, that is until the children do not conform to these. There are many ways in which a child can disappoint or not fulfil their parents wishes, hopes and expectations, such as failing exams, having the wrong friends, not getting married, not having children, or not taking up the expected career.

Some parents are able to deal more easily with their child not conforming to the parental plan. For example, they would not expect their child to take up the career the parents had chosen, or expect them to take over the family business, if they did not want to, even if this is what the parents want.

Although such parents may be unhappy about their child being homosexual they will continue to love and support them and learn to accept it. They are aware that the child must

116

live their own life and be true firstly to themselves, they are aware that no one is happy if they spend their life denying who or what they are and doing what is not right for them. Other parents are shattered by anything their child does, that is not the way they want it to be. They are not aware that their child is a separate person and cannot accept that they are different from the parents. The attitudes of most parents lie somewhere in between.

For all of us, there are things over which we have a choice and in other things we have none. We cannot help the amount of intelligence we have, or perhaps choose our talents, but we can choose how or whether we develop those talents and put them to good or bad use. We can choose to work hard and achieve the best we can and be the best we can be, at whatever we choose to do.

There are things where the personal price for conforming or fitting in with the expectations of others, are just too high. Many are willing to try to do this even though they know that it is denying so much of who they are, how miserable they are and how wrong it feels. For example, it may be following in a family tradition to become a soldier or a doctor, it may be marrying the person the parents like and have chosen, it may be behaving in a traditional heterosexual manner when in fact you are not.

Some take this on for the rest of their lives, making the best of it but suffering inside. Living with the loss of the person they might have become, often becoming stuck in the grieving process for themselves, perhaps remaining bitter or angry. Others do it for a while but eventually are unable to keep up the pretence, wishing to be the person they really are in all areas of their life, to be honest with themselves and others.

This is often seen when someone leaves a good, well paid job to live and work at something far less secure and sensible but which gives them great satisfaction, or when someone decides to come out as a gay man or lesbian woman. At this point they have decided that their honesty and integrity are more important than what others think and feel, even though it may mean losing both family and friends.

A parent fears

For many parents, the idea that their child could be homosexual is horrifying, it is hardly ever mentioned, but the awareness and fear that this could be a possibility is often seen in the behaviour that is not allowed from their children. Even very little boys are discouraged from holding hands, little boys are stopped from dressing up in girls' clothes, girls are discouraged from being 'unfeminine' and sexual stereotyping is encouraged at a very early age. Often the belief seems to be that if such behaviour is stopped, it will prevent the child from developing into a homosexual.

As our children grow up we begin to expect them to behave in certain ways, many parents have been careful to eliminate any signs of effeminate behaviour in their sons or masculine behaviour in their daughters. Other families have a far more relaxed attitude, but however they have been raised some parents will begin to be concerned about the way their child is behaving. They may be behaving in a way that the parents do not see as normal, this could be in their choice of clothes, hobbies, career, or friends.

Their child may be seen as isolated and not mixing with the other children or young people, it may be that word has reached the parents that there has been a lot of name calling and insults aimed at their child. Maybe there are few friends of the opposite sex around, at a time when it is reasonable to expect an interest in the opposite sex to be developing. If all of these do not have a satisfactory explanation, parents may begin to worry.

All to often, the child makes excuses to themselves and their parents, the parents make excuses to themselves and to others, particularly those who ask awkward questions. Everyone has fears and anxieties, questions but no answers and each remains isolated not knowing but not really wanting to know what the truth is, just in case it is what they dread.

In other families, the parents remain unaware that their child is any different to anyone else or themselves. However their child behaves at home, they do not notice, even if their child is unhappy and has tried to talk to them. Parents often assume that their children are only like this at home and are like everyone else when they are elsewhere, that it is just a phase and it will go away or they are to busy with their own life to notice very much about their child's life.

Parents who accept the same prejudices, attitudes, beliefs and judgement that many others in society have, such as, a child will become a homosexual because their parents failed them or because they had a weak father and a dominant mother. That anyone who is gay or lesbian is likely to hurt other people, may lead others astray or turn children or young people into homosexuals. That they are automatically into taking drugs or should not be part of society. If these parents then find out that their child is homosexual they are likely to take all their prejudices on to themselves and their child. Unless they are able to look at their beliefs, they will be unable to find a way of dealing with them.

Although there are many more people who are enlightened, who understand and want the best for their child, for their child to be the person they are, there are very few parents who would receive the news that their child is homosexual, with great delight. They are aware that this is going to make their child's life more difficult, that they will have to face many prejudices both in their work and personal life and that it will affect many areas of their own life, changing the future for all of them.

Finding out

When the truth of the matter is finally known, parents are often horrified and disgusted that their child could be any such thing. Parents often reject their child, sometimes forever, because they are unable to come to terms with who their child is, they may not even be willing to try or they believe that the person who should change is their child. Others reject their child until they are able to come to terms with what has happened and they have gained some understanding, or feel that having a relationship with their child is more important than this.

119

The disgust may be so great that the parents feel unable to even touch their child or allow their child to touch them, the physical reaction may be so bad as to cause the parent to be sick. They are unable to see their child and can only see the person who they feel their child has become. They see their child as they fear and know others will see them and in the way that they view other people who are homosexual.

Parents often feel a lot of guilt, they blame themselves for what has happened, for failing their child, for not doing whatever it is that they were supposed to do to prevent this happening. They believe that if they had realised earlier they would have been able to do something to prevent it happening, believing that this is something that they have control over and they blame themselves for not being more aware.

Some parents are very hurt to discover that their child has been suffering in silence for a long time, trying to conform, trying to be the person they are not. They have felt lonely, confused and isolated, but felt unable to confide in their parents. These parents feel very guilty that their child could not come to them when they had a problem. They feel that they have failed their child and let them down, they now also realise that their relationship with their child was not as they had believed it was.

There are those who will be very unhappy that this could happen without their knowledge, they believed they knew everything about their child and it makes them very insecure to find out that they knew so little. There are those parents who will demand that treatment or a cure is sought or see it as a passing phase or a weakness in their child's personality which has to be eradicated. Some of these parents are willing to put their child through therapies or whatever they feel will put things right, without considering what is in the best interests of their child.

They may believe that their child has become a monster or depraved and will therefore begin to behave in ways that are wrong or wicked. They have believed all the misinformation that they have seen and heard and have forgotten that this is their child who they loved and cherished, who has not just changed in the last few minutes, because the parent now knows. Suddenly the parents are willing to throw away all their past relationship, feeling that it is suddenly invalid because they do not know the person before them as they thought they did.

If the parent has very strong beliefs, maybe supported by their religion, that homosexuality is totally unacceptable, they may find that they cannot reconcile being connected to both their religious beliefs and their child. Their religion is not going to modify its beliefs, the young person is not able to change, so the parent has to make a choice. Either way they are going to lose something that is very important to them and part of their life because their child is different. They are having to make a choice because of something that is totally outside their control, at a time when they are unlikely to be able to make a proper or informed decision.

For parents, one of the main feelings they have to deal with is fear. They are dealing with something that they probably know very little about, they therefore have very little idea of how to deal with it or what to do. There is often a certain amount of fear when we have to deal with something that we do not understand and do not know how to respond to. They fear that their child will die of AIDS, that their child will be attacked or become violent, they fear that they will not be able to get a job or remain in their job and fear that their child will be unable to find happiness.

Life goes on

Once we have truly realised this, we have to find our way and go with it. There are so many questions, many people will go around getting all the information they can to understand more and to discover if there is anything they can do to make things different or to try and find out how to cope with the reactions of themselves and other people.

One of the big questions is who do we tell, when and how? It may be that this is something that can be worked out together and a united front shown to the rest of the world, or there may be differing views, one wanting to keep it quiet and the other wanting or needing to tell other people.

For example, a young man who is gay may have many gay friends from whom he gains support, it is not in his interest for his work to find out so the less people who know, the better. He has decided that his parents should know and has told them but has asked for nobody else to be told. The parents deal with the news in different ways, his mother needs to talk about it, his father refuses, therefore his mother needs to be able to talk to someone.

Who to tell is always a problem, once someone else has been told, it is a secret no longer, there is always the possibility that they will also have the need to tell someone or will let it slip in conversation. Such a piece of information is also the base for such an interesting piece of gossip for those who are not involved and are not on the receiving end of any of the prejudice.

Prejudice against people who are homosexual can also be directed at their families. There will be questions asked about the parents, assumptions made that they were inadequate or their parenting was bad. Their brothers and sisters will have their 'normality' questioned and they will find, at times, they are excluded from things particularly if 'that' brother or sister is likely to be present. Some friends may disappear completely.

This can be for many reasons, some of which can be quite complicated, such as, if they leave their son with you and your gay son is at home, will their son be safe? Are they safe left on their own with your lesbian daughter? How do you talk to someone who is gay? They wonder if it is going to reflect badly on them if they are seen to be connected in any way with someone who is homosexual.

At times the reaction can be violent, gay men, lesbian women and members of their family have been attacked both physically and verbally, received hate mail and their property damaged. All these things create an even greater confusion in the minds of those who are trying to come to terms with what has happened.

When things are going badly or we are suffering from fear of what might happen, it is very hard to hold on to the fact that we are not alone, there is help, advice and support available for the asking and those who create problems are in the minority.

The final decision of who to tell should be in the hands of the person whose life it is, but their hand may be forced by the spread of rumours, by another deciding that they should be 'out', as well as family pressure.

Although it is a very personal matter, it is also affected by changing attitudes in society, pressure groups and the wider debate that is going on to inform, change laws and hopefully encourage people to at the very least allow others to live as they wish as long as it is hurting no-one else.

It is also very difficult not to tell, life is made up of conversations about our families. People regularly ask if you have children, or if you look a suitable age, if you have grandchildren, they ask if your children are married or engaged or have a steady boy or girl friend. It is difficult to avoid giving a straight answer to such questions, if you avoid them people assume that you are being unfriendly, if you tell them the truth it can cause embarrassment, rejection or a whole new set of gossip if you are in a new situation.

Changes for parents

There are a lot of things for these parents to get used to. They are often surprised to find out that they are far more upset about certain things than they ever imagined they would be, things that they did not even realise were important to them. They suddenly find out that they had wanted or expected certain things and now that they are no longer possible, they have to deal with yet another loss. It is important that they are gentle with themselves at this time, what they are upset about probably has many aspects, so it is not a matter of believing that you are being silly, but a matter of grieving for what you have lost and all that it means.

A child who is homosexual will not have the wedding that you had planned or hoped for. If your daughter is lesbian you will not be the mother of the bride, you will not gain a son-in-law. There will be no children from this union but there may be children, if there are, there will always be questions or complications over paternity, even if it is only coping with the ethics of it in your own mind.

There may be also difficulties in coming to terms with your relationship to any children. If your daughter's partner has a baby, then in reality the baby has no relationship to you, for some people this would make it very difficult to accept the baby and their daughter's relationship to it. You are also unlikely to have a true grandchild of your own, if there are any, there is likely to be many other problems.

It could also be difficult to watch your grandchild being brought up in such an unconventional home, it may even be that your daughter has left her marriage, taken her children and gone to live with another woman. It is very difficult for the grandparents to know how to cope with such situations, what to say to the children when they ask questions, never mind other people.

If it is a son who is gay, then there will be no daughter-in-law. Many mothers look forward to having a daughter-in-law with whom to make friends, go shopping with and then to be able to help with the babies. There will be no baby sitting, no taking out the grandchildren. Knowing the fact that there is no guarantee that there would have been grandchildren, even if it had been a heterosexual relationship, and many people hate their son or daughter's partner, does not help one little bit.

Perhaps one of the most difficult things for many parents to come to terms with is their child's partner and their relationship. It is difficult for many parents of heterosexual children to come to terms with their child's sexuality, to accept that they are seeing members of the opposite sex, that they can no longer monitor who their children choose to see and what they do together.

Parents of heterosexual children, can at least have some understanding, by relating their child's behaviour to what they themselves did in their youth, but it is very difficult to do this, when the young person's life, experiences and choices feel and are totally alien to the parent.

It can be very difficult to make a relationship with your child's homosexual friends, when you do not really know what being homosexual means, how is their life different to anyone else, how much of their life does it affect or how they see the rest of us. It can take a long time to be comfortable even in your own home when surrounded by those who feel alien to you and who are often very wary about making any sort of relationship with you.

To accept that your child is sexually mature and that they might be or are sexually active, is not easy. It raises a number of issues such as, their age which reminds us of our age, their youth and freedom which reflects our lack of it, the fact that their childhood and our youth has gone and that we can no longer keep them with us and keep them safe.

It becomes even more difficult when it comes under our own roof. Many parents will not or cannot cope with their heterosexual children sleeping with their opposite sex partners whilst they are in the parents home, even when they have reached adulthood, unless they are married and there can be problems even then. How much more difficult is it then when the partner is of the same sex and marriage is out of the question.

If we love our children we do not want them to be unhappy. Our wish for them was that they should have a good life, a job which they enjoyed, a decent standard of living and that they should have a happy and fulfilling relationship with someone who loved and cared about them and who they loved and cared about.

It is important that we remember what is really important, to celebrate the successes, to encourage the effort, to give love and to recognise and value love, even when it looks a little different to what we expected.

CHAPTER 6

A SERIOUS OFFENDER IN THE FAMILY

For the actions of one, all are made to suffer.
Society wants to blame and have its revenge,
refusing to admit to or think about
the price paid by the innocent.

Hopes and assumptions

We all need our parents to love us and to think that we are wonderful, when we are young we feel and think the same of them. They are the ones in the beginning who teach us right from wrong and how we should be in the world. They are part of us and we get much of the way we feel about ourselves and others from them. It is hard enough to discover that your parents are fallible human beings, how much harder then is it to discover that you have a parent who has committed a horrible offence.

Most people have high hopes when they marry, they believe that the future together is going to be something good and that the person chosen to be with them is reliable, safe and honest. If they have had some problems in their life, at the very least we expect them to leave this behind or to change. We do not expect that they will commit a very serious offence, creating problems for us and giving us a future apart, with them in prison.

As we bring up our children we want to be proud of them, we want them to do better than we did and make their way successfully in the world. They show the world how good we are as parents, we feel that they are our handiwork and we are judged by what people think of them. We do our best often in difficult circumstances to do a difficult job. If we are allowed to celebrate our success when they succeed, can we decide that we had nothing to do with it when they fail?

What would be a serious offence in the eyes of one person will not be to another. If a child is caught shoplifting, to one parent this is the end of the world, all their hopes for the future have come crashing down and they feel that their child's future is ruined and that they will never be able to hold their head up in public again. To another person this is just a part of growing up that the majority of children go through and hopefully, a lesson learned now will prevent more and bigger problems in the future.

Most people have not even visited a court, even less have someone that they are close to face a trial. They would find it very difficult to cope with the idea of someone close to them committing an offence and would have great difficulty coping with it.

For most of us, dealing with a minor traffic offence is traumatic enough, we find it difficult to admit to the truth of what really happened. We find excuses to mitigate the offence, our speedometer was wrong, the weather was bad or the policeman was bored and had nothing better to do, after all no one really did anything 'wrong'.

There are times when it is not that simple, someone has done a serious 'wrong'. It cannot be avoided or excused, perhaps someone has been seriously hurt or has died, or there may have been a lot of damage, or goods and money gone missing. When the offence carries a prison sentence, it is likely to be in the papers, local and, or national and then 'everyone knows'. Everyone will have their own view, judgement about all who are involved and their families and have thoughts about what should be done.

For those who are connected to a person who has committed, or is accused of committing an offence, they have to live with the fact of their connection. This is likely to make life difficult, particularly in the short term but it is unlikely that it will ever completely go away. They will always have to live with the fact that at any time, someone may remember and bring it up again.

A child

If our child has committed a serious offence, it will make a difference to how we feel and deal with it, whether our child is young and still living at home or if they are an independent adult living elsewhere. If they are older, we may be able to claim that they are now responsible for themselves and their actions, but, although they may be responsible for themselves, we are still the ones who brought them up and were supposed to teach them right from wrong. We look back at the upbringing we gave, the childhood they had and question the part we played in it.

All we can teach or do is what we know, we cannot teach or do anything we do not know. We are all a product of our upbringing and it is up to us whether we seek to modify this, learn to be our own person and be the best we can be. Many people do not even think about it and bring their children up in the way that they were brought up, not that they are necessarily aware that they are doing this. Other people try to change and treat their children differently to the way they were treated. Most parents try to do the best they can for their children, very few set out to be bad parents even if this is sometimes what they are.

A child may have had problems for most of their life and their difficulties may have been causing problems from a very young age. They may have been running wild and have been beyond parental control and the troubles they have caused, may have been going on for a long time. There may have been warnings from the police and involvement with drugs and alcohol. They may have mixed in with very bad company and have been influenced by them a lot.

As a parent you may have asked for help, but the help you needed was not given, leaving you feeling very alone, isolated and not coping, but with nowhere to turn for help. There was insufficient support and the other children in the family suffered. This child took up the lion's share of the available time and attention leaving very little for anyone else. The others were probably also treated more severely and were more restricted, in an attempt to try and prevent them doing the same thing, causing them to feel angry and resentful.

It can cause a big split in the family, both their resentment and anger at the way they have been treated by their parents and from the fact that, all the children in the family may well be treated as criminals by other people. They may be excluded, by other people from many situations such as parties, outings and invitations to friends homes. This may make them feel that they have to distance themselves from their sibling and often their family to enable them to have a life in their own right.

The school reports may be bad, they may be average or they may be extremely good, showing a very bright and intelligent student. There may be no awareness at school that there is a problem or that there is likely to be one. The parents may also have an almost perfect child who has not been any trouble or bother and has not caused them a moments worry. The fact that this child has done this is a total shock, causing disbelief and confusion to all who know them.

When it is proved to parents that it is their child who has committed this offence, it may take a long while for the disbelief to go. When it does, the parent is likely to be filled with self-doubt, wondering what they did wrong and what else they should have done. Regretting many things in the past, they feel hurt, let down and confused. They love their child but feel revulsion at what they have done. They may even reject their child along with their rejection of the act that they have committed.

The parents blame themselves, their child and the society who they feel has let their child and themselves down, particularly at this time when so much help and support is needed but much of what they are being given is the opposite.

There is a need to retreat, to think, to try and understand, but this is often not possible because of pressure from the press, hate mail, vicious phone calls and a notable lack of contact, love and support from many of those who should be with and supporting them.

We are aware that the victim is also, someone else's child, just another human being trying to get on with their life. We know that no-one deserves this and have to face the fact that we cannot put this right, we cannot make it better, it has happened and we have to live with this fact and the fact that it was our child who did it.

Our minds may race around trying to find an explanation or an excuse, maybe our child has been framed, maybe they are covering for someone else or maybe the victim did something to cause this to happen. We may become despairing, feeling that we have lost anyway, if the case against them is strong they cannot escape whether they have done it or not.

Our child may be insisting that they are innocent, can we believe them? If they are, why is this happening? All we want is to wake up from this nightmare and find life has returned to normal. There are those parents who feel very angry, not only at their child but at all those who did not do anything to help when they were asked, which would have possibly helped to avoid it coming to this.

There may be a great sense of relief, the parents may feel sorry that this offence has happened to an innocent person, but their child going to prison will for a while remove the worries and anxieties that they have been living with. There is also the hope that at last, something will be done, the necessary help will be given to sort their child out and set them on the right road. This also might be the shock their child requires to make them see where their behaviour is leading them.

A partner

Few people would take on a criminal as a partner, unless they believed that they had changed their ways and that all their bad ways were behind them. Most people believe that the one they have chosen to share their life with is at the very least reasonably, good, honest and kind.

Even if you knew that there was some questionable behaviour in their past, you believed that things would be different when you were both together. You hoped and believed that you would make sufficient difference in their life for them to want to go straight, and that this would be a new beginning. To discover that your partner has then committed a serious offence has probably shattered all your faith and belief in them, in their promises and in the possibility of any sort of life together in the future.

If you had no reason to believe that your partner could ever do anything like this, it will probably shake your faith in people and make it difficult for you to believe in any one. You wonder why you were not aware, what was it about them that you did not see, it is impossible to believe that there was not some way of knowing. You question your relationship, all that you have done together and look for clues.

You become aware of the fact that there were things going on in their life that you had no awareness of, there were parts of their life or personality that you knew nothing about and from which you were left out. You wonder how well you really knew them, how much you were separate when you thought that you were together and question your ability to know or understand anyone.

You consider their family, should there have been some clues there. If their family were not completely honest or good, you had been fooled into believing that your partner was different from the rest of them, you feel that you have been very gullible and stupid. Maybe there was no reason to suspect anything at all, because their family life was sound, good and honest. No matter what the situation is, you probably still feel that somehow you should have realised or been aware of the possibility that this could happen.

There is not only the disbelief that something like this has come near you, there is also the disbelief that this could have been done by a person you love and care about. In a matter of domestic violence, it may even be to you that the offence has been committed. Even when the evidence is this clear, we often try to explain it away, blame ourselves or put it down to an unfortunate set of circumstances. We do not want to believe that this has happened and who has done it.

If we were not there when it happened, we were not part of it, we do not really know what occurred and only know what we have heard or been told. It is very hard to believe or imagine that a person we love, could do such a thing. It can be equally hard to believe that they did not do it, when the evidence against them is strong. How can we look the one we love in the eye and ask them if they did this dreadful thing? How can we admit that we do not believe them or have doubts when they are protesting their innocence? If we defend them are we defending an innocent person or assisting a dangerous person to remain in society?

We want to hide and protect the one we love, even if we have doubts, we do not want to admit that the one the police are looking for sounds very much like the one we know. We do not want to be part of this or even consider that this is happening to us, this only happens in novels or on the news. How can we consider handing over our partner and bringing the nightmare that is happening to someone else, into our own life.

What will happen if I do this, will I be throwing the police and the authorities yet another helpless victim or will I be serving justice. Do I tell and be the creator of my own punishment, or, if I do not tell what I know, will I then be the one committing a crime.

A parent
At some stage in our lives we need to admit that our parents are human beings with faults, this can come to some children as rather a shock and they may try to deny it or respond by putting their parent on a pedestal. We discover that our parents are just like other people and that their failings make

them human, it is often a long time before we allow them to be like anyone else. Eventually we deal with this and then become equally uncomfortable with them when they appear to be different to other people.

It is altogether another matter when our parents really are different to others and making it even more difficult for us to be like everyone else. If they are more rich or more famous it is hard enough to deal with but, if they have committed a serious offence it is nearly impossible.

It may be hard to be the daughter of a pop star with an unusual act, but there are always those who would like to be your friend, you can always name-drop and get to meet interesting people (and take a friend). What is written in the papers about them may not always be complimentary, but you can laugh about it together. What can you do to cope with what is written in the newspapers about a criminal father, who will want to be your friend (or be allowed to be) and, what benefits can there ever be?

It is nearly impossible for a child to develop a relationship with a parent who is in prison for a long time. There is very little contact that they can have, problems cannot be talked through, understanding cannot be developed and they cannot be an ongoing, physical presence in each others' lives. A child may feel that they have to defend their parent against the world, or join with the world in condemning them.

How does a child reject a parent when they need their parent to love them? How do they reject this part of themselves? How do they support the parent at home, through their problems and grief and not hate the parent who has caused this pain and difficulty for them all?

How can a child believe anything that has been taught to them by a parent who can do such a wicked deed? Or is it the rest of society who is wicked for blaming them? How can a child know what is right either in their own life or in the large outside world? They have been rejected by a parent who has left them to go to prison and consequently are living in a world that is in many ways also rejecting them. It was up to the parent to do what is right, not what is wrong, thereby causing all this hurt to the family they should be caring for and protecting.

Many children believe, rightly or wrongly, that their parent is innocent and they wonder why their parent has been taken from them. Because they have lost so much, their family may have fallen apart, money is short and there are many difficulties. They often feel that something is seriously wrong with society, the society that they are being expected to grow up into and take part in, the society who is supposed to care for them and their family.

Whatever our age we still want the love and approval of our parents, we also want to love and approve of them, to be proud of them and feel able to tell anyone about them or take anyone home to them. In any family this is not always easy to achieve, but if a parent has committed a serious offence, not only will it be very difficult to know what we want from them anymore, it will be very difficult to talk about them, take anyone home or admit a connection.

Whatever our relationship to the offender, we do not want to believe that they have done this or believe it was their fault. We look for a scapegoat, someone to blame. Perhaps they had some bad experiences or work pushed them too hard. Maybe the victim did something wrong and they are not totally innocent, maybe they started it, or perhaps someone else was to blame.

In some cases, the offender is mentally ill. The family have probably been doing all they can for a very long time, without the help and support that they should be receiving. They know that their relative was not responsible for their actions and for what they have done, but this rarely stops the family from feeling responsible. They feel that they should have done more even when more could not have been done. They feel caring and protective towards their relative at the same time as being revolted at what they have done. They may receive some support from others, but they still have to face and cope with the revengeful part of society and those who will question their sanity.

Family and friends

The reactions of other members of the family and of friends will depend on many things, such as the quality of the relationship they had with the offender, other members of their family and the nature of the offence. There is a big difference between choosing to remain friends with a fraud or remaining friends with a rapist.

Some people will feel that they are unable to have any further contact with the offender, but feel able and in fact want to remain friends with members of their family and are willing to give their help and support. Many people find it difficult to understand why members of the family still continue to care about the offender, to keep in contact with them and visit them in prison.

Often pressure is put on them to stop visiting and having contact, particularly if the visits and contact cause upset and distress. Some family members will want to have nothing to do with the offender because of what they have done, others because they find the contact, particularly the prison visiting, very distressing.

Remaining friends can cause difficulties in other areas of life. Other people do not understand how you can face having any contact and may assume that because you have this contact you are in fact not much better than the offender. It is often very difficult to remain totally honest and true to yourself. It can be much easier to say that you continue to have contact because you felt sorry for the family or that you could not avoid the family because of family ties, rather than admit the fact that you care and want to have the contact.

Being honest can lead to being criticised or avoided. At times there may be more aggressive behaviour towards yourself or you may be thought of by condescending people, as someone who is being very brave, kind and doing a good deed.

There are those people who will appear to be helpful, caring and supportive in private but will denounce the family in public. They may use information they have gained from

135

inside the family to get attention from anyone who will listen, showing that they have the 'inside' story. They may even tell the press what they know and use this platform to get attention and to give their views and opinions about the offender and their family to the world.

What has to be faced

For anyone to discover that someone they care for has committed a serious offence is a dreadful shock. Whilst they are trying to cope with this, there are many other things happening at the same time. One of the things that is very difficult to grasp and to cope with, is that when someone is arrested, they are immediately taken away before what is happening is grasped and the implications realised. From this point on, until they are released, there is no say or control over contact with them, it is all organised and decided by those in authority. There will not be any opportunity to speak in private or even have a few moments alone.

A plea for just a few more moments, for just another word together, for time to try and make sense of what is happening, is rarely allowed. In shock it is almost impossible to believe that this is happening. It may be understood why it is necessary for the police to search our house but it induces a sense of helplessness, a sense of being taken over.

Our most personal and private possessions are being handled by uncaring strangers, who we do not want to touch our belongings. We feel that our very being is being invaded, there is no corner left unturned and we feel raw and exposed. Nothing is sacred, nothing is left untouched, there is no part of our home that is left unviolated.

Our personal life has become public. Statements are made by all sorts of people about not only the offender but also about ourselves, questions are asked of many people about what sort of people we are, what is our life like, what do we do and what we have got. Our life is up for public scrutiny and it feels as though anyone who wishes, can have a say. Nothing is too private or secret, all will be revealed.

We are watched, maybe by the police, but definitely by other people, we wonder what other people are saying about us, how can it be anything but awful when such a dreadful deed has been done. We know this because we have all joined in conversations about others, commenting about who had seen them, how they looked, what they were doing and what, if anything, they said, then passing our own judgement about what this means.

What do we say to people, family, friends and people we meet? is it ever going to be easy to talk and meet with others again? Will there ever be another thing in our lives? Can we ever leave it behind? This thing has happened, it will never go away, to some extent we will have to live with this for the rest of our lives. We will always have another label now – the parent, partner, relative or whatever, of the person who committed that dreadful act – "you remember the one who ..." and so the story lives on.

To others in our family we have to give support and help them realise that whatever they choose to do, this is now part of their lives and there will always be those who will judge them because of it. Our friends who stick with us have to realise that they also run the risk of being tarred with the same brush.

How do we make people realise that we may hate what the person has done, but love cannot just be switched off and that we still love the person. We need time to try and understand, what has happened and why, how we feel about them and the offence, so that we can decide what to do. We have to be open enough to allow other members of the family also, to do what is right for them.

Anyone, but in particular family members, may be vilified, have to cope with acts of vandalism to their property, receive hate mail and have abusive telephone calls made to them. Sometimes members of their family are attacked and it seems that there is no way of being totally protected. Their lives may be filled with fear and they are driven away from the place where they live, but if they move away, there will always be the question of whether anywhere else will be safe as soon as anyone discovers who they are.

The people who are being victimised, are being punished for being married or related to someone who has committed a horrible offence. This is their crime and they will pay for it, society will attempt to get its' revenge. It cannot reach the person who has done this thing so will get their family. There is also a lot of curiosity. Not only a need to know how anyone could do this or why, but a wish to know all the grisly details, if only to say how sick it made them feel.

Innocent until proven guilty

This may be so in law, but it will not be necessarily so in many peoples' minds. Rightly or wrongly, lack of belief in their innocence may be held by some of the police investigating the offence, people we know and wider society. They may have made up their minds from what they hear on the news or read in the papers. It may even be ourselves who do not believe in their innocence.

Society feels safe in its' self righteousness, believing that the person taken in for questioning or the person who has been arrested must have done it or this would not be happening to them. Therefore there are those who feel justified in attacking them, their families and their property before anything has been proved. Many people who are later proved to be totally innocent or have just been to the police station to answer questions, return home to frightened families and vandalised homes.

It may be hard to believe in either the person's guilt or their innocence. If we believe in their innocence, it takes a lot of courage to stand up, maybe against everyone else, including the judicial system to defend them and continue with a fight for justice, their freedom and acquittal.

Often there is a wish to believe that they are innocent, yet an actual belief that they are guilty, this is very difficult to cope with if they are insisting that they are innocent. It is an added betrayal if we defend them and then later they admit to committing the offence.

If you have decided to stick with them, you will not only have the pain of your own distress, anxieties and doubts, but also of watching fairly helplessly, as they try to deal with their distress at what has happened, at the way they have been treated, at their loss of freedom and all that this means.

If they are innocent there may be their inability to get anyone to believe it, if they are not innocent the distress may be caused by the guilt at what they have done. There is also the problem of time, it takes so long to find out anything, for decisions to be made or for the case to come to court as the wheels of justice move extremely slowly.

It may be that they have committed the offence but are not sorry, it is very difficult to cope with their lack of guilt at what they have done. This can make you feel confused and distanced from them, it can also make you feel very guilty, not only for the offence but because they do not feel sorry, which can make it feel like your failure. If you fail in getting them to feel sorry, often there is the feeling that the only way to cope with these feelings of guilt and failure is for you to attempt to make reparations yourself.

We may be trying to believe them but it is sometimes very difficult. Often we have lost the trust and faith we had in them, we may have discovered things that we did not know and things that we do not like (probably the reason we did not know in the first place). All of which, make us realise that we do not know this person as well as we thought. If we have doubts about their innocence or have found out about other things that worry us, we wonder if there have been other things done and other, possibly worse offences committed.

There is also the possibility of having to give evidence in court. This can be a terrifying and traumatic experience, even if the testimony you have to give is that which you are happy to give. The whole experience is frightening and the most straightforward evidence, in the hands of a barrister, can be made to sound like the basis of some devilish plot.

Sitting through a trial can be very painful and having to remain quiet when what is happening seems unfair is very difficult. There will be things said that you do not want to hear and the pain of the victim, their family and friends will be difficult to cope with. They are wishing for a guilty verdict to help ease their pain, you want an innocent verdict to ease yours.

Some of your punishment

You may feel that you have been punished enough already, but now that the court has made its decision and they have been sent to prison, life has to settle down and somehow, a way forward has to be found. There are many problems to deal with and questions to answer. The most immediate will probably be the practical ones such as, what income do we have? What about jobs and schools? Can we afford to continue to live here and if we do not want to, can we afford to move?

The media attention may be off now or at least for the present and we may have helpful and supportive friends and neighbours, so we may wish to remain where we are. But it may be, that after all that has happened a fresh start is needed, somewhere new where we are not known.

The make-up of the family is going to be different, there is one away who will miss all the family things that are happening, like birthdays, holidays and Christmases. We may feel very sad or very angry about this. Either at the justice system, because you feel that justice has not been done or the person themselves for what they have done and are consequently putting you through. There will be family members who miss them and want to think and talk about them, whilst others will not want them mentioned. So many innocent people are punished for what someone else has done.

It is painful for you to have them taken and kept away from you, but this is their punishment. However, it may be even more difficult to cope with them rejecting you, saying that they do not want any further contact with you. This may be for many reasons. They may feel that you would be better off just getting on with your lives without them, they may feel that because they are not physically in your life they should go completely, thinking that you can just switch them off in your thoughts.

It may be that they feel that you have let them down, because of the evidence you gave or the way you gave it, because they feel you should have done more or because they think or believe that it was you that gave them away. Whatever the reasoning, there is little you can do, their right not to be in contact with you will be upheld by the authorities, whose job it is to support and protect the prisoner. You on the other hand must get on without this protection and support and you have very little option other than to do what is asked.

Now that the verdict has been given and life must go on, friends and family have to perhaps think more clearly about where they stand on this matter and in your life from here. They have many of the same issues to deal with in their own minds and it may take a while before they know what they think or feel or before they are able to know what they want to do. Often it will be up to you to help them through this by being there for them and either giving them the opportunity to talk it through or the space to work it out for themselves.

Some of the family will want you to get on with your life, others will want your life, like theirs to stand still until the end of the prison sentence. There will be equally differing views on most other issues, including what everyone should do at the end of the sentence and how you should cope and deal with this.

Contact with the prisoner

Most of the time that they are in prison you may fear for their safety. Will they be attacked? Will they be encouraged to use drugs? Will you know whether they are having problems or not? Are they being victimised or becoming depressed? Will they receive sufficient help, care and protection whilst they are in prison or will they just have to suffer in silence?

A decision has to be made about whether to visit or not, the whole idea is very distressing, but if you do not visit you will not be able to tell if they are getting better or worse. If they are getting worse, will it be your fault for not visiting? It will also be impossible to know what is happening to them.

It is very difficult to know how to keep them as part of the family. Not only keeping them informed about what is going on and keeping yourself informed about their life, but how to keep them feeling as though they are still part of what is happening and keep them involved.

They are in a different world to those of us outside and it is only through the limited contact that is allowed, that these two worlds can attempt to remain in contact. There is a lot of opportunity for each to imagine that the others' world and life is different to what it is and what they are being told, this can lead to distrust and misunderstandings which are difficult to cope with and overcome.

Prison visiting is difficult and can be difficult in so many ways. Just arranging to visit can be challenging, sometimes involving long journeys to a strange town, organising child-minding and time off work. When you get there it may be necessary to queue on the street, to be gazed at by passers by, before you get in and then there is the indignity of being searched. Understanding of why these things have to be done, does not necessarily make us feel any less uncomfortable with them.

However glad you may feel to see them, it is always a sad occasion. So much to say and so much difficulty in saying it, so much fear of being misunderstood or of causing the other worry and concern, when at the end of the visit they return to their life and you journey back to yours. If it is a long journey and the weather is cold and wet it is difficult not to become resentful. They at least are warm and dry.

It is hard not to pour out all your problems and difficulties but that would waste the time, but what can you say when you are not able to relax and say whatever you want. If they are having problems and difficulties, your feelings are likely to be mixed, you are concerned for them, resentful that they are moaning when they have done this to themselves and feel that they are probably having an easier time than you managing on your own at home.

The conversation can be strained, the resentment about what they have done to you and the family can hang between you and it takes a while for the barriers to be overcome and to be able to relax and talk to one another again. Then it is time to leave, to feel sad at parting, guilty about the lack of support you have given, resentful at the lack of support they gave you and at the lack of privacy. So much said that no-one intended to say, so little said that was intended, all too often it feels as though yet again the opportunity has been wasted and it is so long to the next one.

For so many people, visiting someone they care about in prison is a dreadful ordeal, they feel themselves drifting apart through lack of contact, but feel unable to establish sufficient contact when they visit. They watch the changes in them, their moods, manner and attitude, there is a growing apart as they change and adapt to their new world, which you are not and cannot be part of.

Decisions and fears for the future

We may need to spend time thinking about whether we are or whether we are not in any way to blame for what has happened. If we are the parent, was it a fault in our parenting? As a partner or a child, was it anything that we did, or did not do that contributed to the offence happening?

It is only by taking full responsibility for ourselves and our own actions, that we can begin to deal with our guilt. It is only when we have decided what blame, if any, is attached to us, can we rid ourselves of the feelings of guilt and responsibility for all those things that are not our fault, that we had no part in and were not responsible for.

We need to rid ourselves of all those things that are not ours and do not belong to us, put them where they belong and then get on with our own life. We can then begin to look at what we really want and to make the decisions we want. If we are carrying all sorts of guilt and responsibilities that do not belong to us, we will only be able to make decisions that relate to these. We will not be able to make decisions that are for ourselves and our own future.

Many of the decisions and choices we have to make are very difficult and often it is very unfair that we have to make them, but it is important that we make the ones we want, we are the ones who are going to live with them. Decisions such as; are we going to move? Are we going to stick with the offender? Are we going to have them back when they have finished their sentence?

Although we may have to modify our decisions to some extent, perhaps because of the responsibility we have for our children, it is still very important that we make the decisions that are right for us and that we can cope with. If they are right for us, we will be able to care for our children and support them through it.

There is also the fact that life and people change. Everything may look very different at the end of a long sentence from what it did at the beginning. Many of the intentions and plans we had at the beginning, may not have been carried out, children grow up and leave home to get on with their own lives and our responsibilities change. The people we were then are not who we are now, we have not lived, grown or worked together or shared the same life, responsibilities or experiences.

Any decisions we make, can only be the best that we can make now, with the information that is available now. There are so many things we do not know, cannot know or plan for. We are also only part of the equation, we may have control over our-self and what we will do, but we cannot have control over another person. We cannot make decisions for another person, as we do not really know what they truly want or will fully agree to. We can only truly make decisions for our-selves and our own lives.

There are many questions and fears we may have such as, will they commit more offences in the future? Will they want to come back to us? Will they settle and cope with an ordinary life? It is difficult to know whether they will be accepted back into society, be able to get a job or perhaps be blighted for life.

They, like us must make their own decisions and take responsibility for themselves, their past and their future actions. When we have each learned the life lessons we have faced and grieved for our losses, only then, when we really know what we truly want, will we be able to help one another to work out what is the best way forward for all concerned.

PART 3

EFFECTS ON OTHERS

We need to be aware, that these things have an effect on others.
They need to be aware, that this is happening to us.
Only then, can we help one another.

CHAPTER 1

SIBLINGS; IMMEDIATE AND LATER EFFECTS

So often they are close to the special one, connected but different.
Slightly in their shade, they are the ones,
who hold their families' hopes and expectations.

A problem sibling or a sibling with a problem

Most of us would say at one time or another as we grew up, that our siblings were a problem. Those without any siblings, at times wish that they had some and those with siblings would gladly hand them over. Over the years our attitudes and relationships change towards each other as we each become our own person, connected but separate from each other and our family.

Whatever age we are, we remain siblings. Whether we are close, have contact, are friends or not. When we grow up we are still brothers and sisters, over this fact and connection we have no choice. Our relationship or lack of it has been built up over the years and affected by many things.

Any individual is profoundly affected by a bereavement, with or without a death, so are their family, not only all of its' members but also the relationships between the members. We do not choose our brothers and sisters and usually have little say in their lives, but we are none the less affected, often deeply, by what happens to them.

What happens in the life or to the life of one child in a family, can have a life changing effect on all the members. This is particularly true of the child's siblings who are

149

growing up and coping with difficulties during their formative years.

A child who is younger than a sibling with disabilities or, one who is having or causing difficulties, is often born into the situation. If this is so, life is the way it has always been and it is possibly more easy to accept the way things are, including accepting their older sibling for who and what they are. They may however, have difficulty giving up the status of being the youngest or the one requiring most attention. This is hard when it is given up to a younger child but even harder when it is given up to an older brother or sister, whatever the reason.

For an older sibling, there was a time before there were all these problems and difficulties. It is difficult enough accepting a new brother or sister, but it is especially hard when they arrive and take up all the time and attention. It may be that, for all the family there were no great problems for years but suddenly this has happened and this child has taken the lion's share of everyone's time and attention. The parents become stressed and anxious having no time or patience, suddenly this child has taken over and changed everything.

Both at the time and later, these things cause a mixture of feelings, which are felt differently at every age and stage. These feelings are difficult to cope with and if expressed, can receive a very unsympathetic reception, increasing the sense of guilt already felt. There is a feeling of helplessness as this is not happening to me but it is affecting me and my life and there is nothing I can do about it. There is a feeling of gratitude that it is happening to them and not to me, a sense of superiority that I am fine and they are not and feelings of jealousy for all the attention and things they are getting that I am not.

Although life eventually settles down, it settles down in a way that becomes normal for that family but not the way that anyone in the family would have chosen or wanted. What has happened has to some extent permanently changed the life of the family, each of its members and their relationship to one another.

Some of the problems and difficulties

Many of the problems and difficulties are caused by others, such as those who assume that somehow you must be affected by the same problem as your sibling or that you must also be bad or have great difficulties. If your sibling has a learning disability, they assume that you must also have difficulties, or if your sibling is violent they assume that you must also have violent tendencies or be a passive victim.

It almost seems as though it is OK to insult you or probe into your life but what usually happens is that you are ignored whilst your brother or sister gets all the attention, gifts and help. There are often different expectations of you than of other people. For example, it is often assumed that those with a brother or sister with disabilities will be more caring and understanding, more willing to put their sibling and others first and be willing and able to do whatever is required.

For many children who have a sibling with special needs or siblings who have other problems and difficulties, there are often different sets of rules within the family. One set for them and a different set for their sibling. Frequently parents are not aware that they are making these differences between their children, or they assume that this is the way things have to be. Often they cannot manage to make the necessary effort to maintain the same set of rules for all.

Even where the same rules are applied to all the children, often the application has to be or is different to allow for differing abilities and temperaments. Frequently it is assumed that this will just be accepted without question and that there will be automatic understanding of why things are done the way they are.

For these siblings there are many losses, loss of a carefree childhood, the loss of many treats and outings and of time and attention from parents and others. All too often there is not the time to do what they want or the space in which to do it. For some, their sibling is often ill or they have appointments to attend and very often parents just do not have the energy. No matter what they want to do, it always seems that somehow their 'special' sibling manages to spoil it. Even as an adult, 'they' still manage to take up most of the available time and attention within the family.

Carer siblings are usually more mature for their age, having had to take more responsibility than their peers, either caring and watching out for their brother or sister or helping out whilst their parents are dealing with them or the results of what they have done. They often live in a situation where it is difficult to know what to expect from minute to minute or what plans will be changed at the last moment. It is often embarrassing or difficult to bring friends home, the different life experience and expectation can make it difficult to fit in with others or be part of a peer group.

They also often feel and take on a lot of responsibility for their parents, worrying about them, watching their pain and feeling helpless. To be of what help they can, they often do not ask for what they need or want (not realising that this often causes their parent more worry), they try to cope with things on their own and consequently often do not learn to value themselves or their needs. These problems do not only arise when they are young, grown-up siblings often still have the same worries and concerns. They still need the time and attention of a parent or friend, to listen to them, to care and give them support.

As we grow up, we carry many of the behaviours, thoughts and feelings with us that we have learned. For those with brothers and sisters who have dominated their childhood with their problems, these thoughts and feelings can vary from jealousy of anyone who has more than they have to anger at the world. From a need to be noticed to a fear of upsetting anyone, from having a career in the caring services to being unable to say no to any request for help.

Problems with children put a lot of strain on marriages. Where there are many problems and there have been losses, many marriages do not survive. For these children there is a much greater chance that along with what they have already lost, they will also have to cope with the break-up of their parents' marriage. Frequently this means that they now have to live with one parent, who is trying to cope with all the things that previously, two parents had difficulty managing.

To add to their problems, these children also have pressure, sometimes from parents, sometimes they put the pressure on themselves, to fulfill their parents' hopes for themselves, their children and their future. This may be to have a brilliant career, to provide the longed for grandchildren or somehow make up for what has been lost in their family. It is very difficult, for these parents to enable and allow their children to be who they are and the children to feel free, to live the way they want and to be who and what they truly wish to be.

A sibling of a child with a learning disability

Very often, siblings of a child with disabilities, feel that they and their families are different from other people and their life is also not like that of others. As they grow up, they are often helped by the opportunity to mix with other children in the same position as themselves. Meeting and talking to other children, young people and adults who have a brother or sister with disabilities, allows them to share experiences, discuss their common problems and enables them to feel less isolated. Unless this is arranged for them, there is rarely the opportunity in their everyday lives, to meet others in the same position.

There is an enormous lack of appreciation of just how much life is affected by having a brother or sister with disabilities. For an older sibling it means, not only have they had their light eclipsed but from here on, so much is expected of them, from the expectation that they will be successful, to the expectation of the help they will give.

For a younger sibling, this brother or sister was always there, they will often be expected to make the family feel optimistic about the future again. They will also be expected to make good progress themselves, to overtake their sibling and encourage their progress, to give up their status as youngest and becoming a playmate, teacher and minder.

These siblings are expected to be willing, patient and caring. It is often assumed that they are automatically happy to be involved in the care, supervision, minding, teaching and play of their disabled sibling. They often have difficulty keeping their possessions safe and undamaged, they give up a lot of their time and often find it difficult to have very much privacy or freedom.

It is often hard for a child who has a sibling with a disability to feel that they are important and that they count. At home, usually out of necessity, the child with the disability is the centre of attention, to keep them safe, to help them along and for the family to cope with all the demands that this child and his needs makes on them.

Away from home, they are often considered to be very cute, but their disability frequently makes people feel uncomfortable. The special needs child will often be given gifts and attention, whilst their siblings, even the younger ones, are there and totally ignored, given nothing and hushed by an embarrassed parent if they protest.

The special needs child will often be given many treats that their siblings do not get, such as parties, outings and gifts. These things cannot be balanced by parents, often they could not afford to, even if they could it would be an artificial situation and therefore unsatisfactory. These situations mainly come from outside the family, for example, a special needs child will come home from school at the end of term with sweets, chocolates and gifts, a mainstream child will come home with a card from their teacher. It is very difficult to tell a child that when they grow up things will balance out and for them to accept the unfairness of it.

It is not surprising that siblings become jealous at times, particularly when their brother or sister has been given a treat, outing or opportunity that they have wanted and longed for but cannot have, such as riding lessons or a visit to the theatre. This understandable jealousy is very hard to cope with, along with their added problem of feeling guilty for feeling this way.

It is hard coping with the mixture of feelings about and for a brother or sister who has disabilities. They are probably in a worse position than you and have problems and difficulties that you do not, but although it is through no fault of their own, they have at times been difficult. They are your sibling who you love and care for but who is also able drive you just as mad as any other sibling can. The loving, caring and protective feelings are in direct opposition to the feelings of resentment, jealousy and anger.

It is very sad to hear a sibling stopped and told off when they express some of these difficult feelings. Most people find it acceptable for a child to say they hate a brother or sister or call them things like stupid and ugly. It is called sibling rivalry and is a normal part of growing up, it is possibly a sign of emotional health and is often seen as cute or funny by those around them. The reaction to a child saying the same things about a sibling with a learning disability is often one of horror. It is difficult living with a sibling to whom and of whom you are not allowed to express your real feelings.

It is an unhappy situation when parents have not come to terms with their own feelings about their child sufficiently, to be able to allow their other children to express their own feelings. These sibling are often told that they are bad to feel the way they do or should not say things like this. They then feel guilty and believe that they are bad, instead of being able to just have as normal a relationship as possible with their brother or sister, who is also consequently being denied this opportunity.

Other people, outside the immediate family, also find it very difficult to hear anything except how cute and loving the child with special needs is or how tragic and sad it all is. It is not only the dead who cannot have ill spoken about them.

If a sibling or even a parent, tries to tell of something the disabled child did that is not good or funny and perhaps tries to say how it really is they are unlikely to receive a warm reception. They may well be faced with a person, who will try not only to change the sibling's attitude, insist that things are the way that they wish to believe they are or will just refuse to listen seriously.

It is very difficult for these siblings to cope with the feelings they have toward their brother or sister. Many find it hard to express their feelings and even more difficult to find a person who understands their situation or who has enough understanding to allow them, not only to express their feelings but also to explore them and find out what they really are. If they and their feelings can be accepted, they are enabled to work through their very real and natural feelings of anger, hate, frustration, grief and loss.

Some of the problems

The problems caused by a child with disabilities, touch on most areas of family life. The children have to deal not only with a brother or sister with disabilities, but also parents who are having their own problems dealing with the situation. This often leaves the parents short of energy. Frequently, family life is restricted because of the needs, abilities and disabilities of the special needs child and also what parents feel that they can cope with.

At times, parents insist that they are and should behave just like a 'normal family' and do the things that other families do, like going out for a meal. To the siblings it is quite obvious, to them and to the rest of the world, this is not so. The whole exercise is often inappropriate and very embarrassing for them. Such things may cause a lot of tension and difficulty in the family, each member having their own view about what is embarrassing, appropriate or OK.

It is difficult enough to be seen with parents at certain ages and stages. How much more difficult to also be accompanied by this brother or sister who may behave inappropriately, be disruptive, take everyone's attention and even upstage you when you should be the star for once in your life, such as on your special occasion.

To have your disabled brother or sister left out, when all the family should be there, is also unthinkable. There are also those times when you want to stand proudly alongside your sibling, be seen by the world and say this is mine, 'haven't they done well, haven't I done well, haven't we all done well?'.

Often it is difficult to bring new friends home, because the people we bring home may not know how to respond to our special needs sibling. They may be embarrassed by them or not know how to deal with the situation. Some people find someone with a learning disability threatening and others do not know how to cope with someone who has difficulty communicating. At other times it is difficult to be left alone with friends without the sibling joining in, siblings are aware that it is very difficult for their brother or sister to have friends or be able to see them away from school. They feel guilty if they do not include them but fed up or angry if they have to.

There are many expectations of the sibling of a child with special needs. They are the ones who are expected to have a 'normal' life because they have the benefit of not having any major disabilities. They are expected to make a success of their life, on them hangs not only the hopes of the family's future but the hope that they will make it sufficiently good to make everyone feel that life is in fact OK.

Frequently there is the assumption, not only from their families but by society in general, that they will be their sibling's helpers, not only now but for the rest of their lives. This is a difficult problem, often whilst they are young, this is what siblings want to do and would feel very guilty and possibly also resentful, if they were to consider doing otherwise. As they grow up and begin the move away from home, it is essential that siblings have the opportunity and permission to move away, live their own life and to develop their own careers and relationships.

It is often a difficult thing for them to do, they may need help and support to separate themselves to some degree, from the problems, difficulties or unsatisfactory situation that they feel they are leaving behind and believe they should be staying to help. It is often difficult for parents to let one of their main helpers go and perhaps face a more restricted life themselves. Being aware of this, the children may need an encouraging push.

Perhaps the most difficult problems are that a brother or sister with a severe disability often dies young and it is likely that siblings will have to cope with their death. If they do not die, then there is the problem of what siblings should do with their brother or sister after the death of the parents.

Often it is not realised that this is a big worry for siblings, from a very early age. It is also a very difficult subject to raise or talk about, particularly with parents or other siblings because it is about death, the death of the brother, sister or parents. It is often a subject that each member of the family avoids but that each member of the family worries about, wants to talk about and to have some answers to the questions; How will I cope if they die? What will happen to them when I die? What will I do when my parents die?

These difficult questions have the potential for causing a lot of distress and disagreement, it is even more difficult to raise and discuss them with anyone else, except perhaps those in the same situation. They do need to be addressed if lives are to be lived and moved forward. Each member of the family needs some idea of what to expect and what is expected of them.

A sibling of an adult with Alzheimer's disease

How much affect this may have on you and how much you are involved, depends on many things, such as, how much contact you have with each other, what age you both are, how much you like them and how near to them you live. You could also be affected by how much you are worried about whether you might also develop this disease, therefore you may be seeing what might happen to you in the future.

Although Alzheimer's is mainly a disease of older people, it can happen to those who are relatively young and are still bringing up their children. If this is the case, you probably will also be in the midst of bringing up your own children and developing your own career. Your life is probably very busy with its own ups and downs and problems and there is very little space to cope with such a large, time consuming, long term problem.

Even when we are older, we are probably still very busy or feel that we deserve a little space and relaxation, therefore, most people will feel that they have very little time or space to cope over the long term that this disease requires. We have to question where our loyalties lie and our own families need our time, help and attention. We have our own relationships to take care of and we also need some space in our lives for ourselves.

We have to consider our priorities, look at our lives and face our feelings of guilt at being less kind, helpful and generous than we like to admit. We also have to face our feelings about what has happened, the tragedy of the disease and what it is doing and going to do to our brother or sister and their family. Our own feelings about what has happened to them, often has a sobering effect on us, as we look at our own lives and how we are living them, as we consider our own health, strength and mortality and that of those we love.

How we feel and respond to our brother or sister and their family, how it has affected us, what we think and decide to do, depends usually on the relationship we had in the past and the one we have now with both them and their family. These are also likely to affect how we discovered what was happening, whether we had any warning that there were problems or were suddenly and unexpectedly faced with the diagnosis. If we are in regular contact and see them often, we are likely to have seen some of the problems, the differences in moods, behaviour and ability, we are also likely to have heard the concerns of those around them. On the other hand, if we rarely see them and have little contact, we may not realise that there are any problems at all.

If you are close to your brother or sister and are happy to help with their care, being able to do this may help you cope better with the loss and help you to feel that you have at least, done all that you could to help. On the other hand, if you do not like them or have very little contact, the feelings are likely to be very different. Sometimes there is a wish to put things right before it is too late, but if they have become confused, this may be difficult, leaving their sibling not knowing whether this has been accomplished or not.

It may be that the rift has become so big that you do not care, or are not willing to do anything to help. Although you may choose for this to be the case, there may be feelings of regret and a wish that things might have been different. There may be regret at the loss of the relationship and a sadness that life turned out this way, if you tried to reach out and had been rejected, you may feel angry and that perhaps they have got what they deserve.

However you have felt and whatever your relationship has been with your brother or sister, gradually they will go, leaving behind a person who no-one knows, who still has to be cared for. If you live close by it may be that you will be expected to help. This may be something that you are happy to do, or it may leave you feeling that you have been totally lumbered with something you do not want to do, be part of or have the time and energy to do. This can result in feelings of resentment, anger at them, their family, society and the world.

You may have strong feelings about the role of your children in this situation, as they are their nephews and nieces, should they be expected to help? Do you interfere if you are unhappy about the amount of help they are giving or are expected to give or do you stand back and allow them their own relationship with their uncle or aunt, regardless of your relationship with them.

It is difficult to know how much help to give, it will always feel either too much or too little and never be enough for the amount of help required. It is likely that you will feel some guilt whatever you do and often you will try to resolve this in terms of what is your duty. There will also be many thoughts about what others are doing to help or not doing. Are they doing as much as they should or as much as you are? Are they fulfilling their duty? Do they think you are fulfilling yours? This is the basis for many family arguments, fights and resentments which are often never resolved, each person becoming entrenched in their own corner.

Often it is difficult to know what to do. If you are involved in their care, you may not like what their family is doing and how they are doing it. Being one removed, it is difficult to feel part of the group and often you will have no say in what is happening. You may feel that it is not your place to say what you think or to do so would create difficulties in your relationship with others in the family.

Many of the early acute feelings will modify and soften over the years. As things change there will be opportunities for bridges to be built, love, care and affection to be shown and a sense of family or community built up. On the other hand, it may be felt that it is their problem, we all went our separate ways a long time ago, we all have our own lives to lead and that is what we all should do.

A sibling of an adulterer

Most of us have mixed feelings about our siblings and about the values we were brought up with but we do have certain beliefs and expectations. Often we do not know what these are until they are challenged. As we grow up we learn that life is not very pleasant at times, we know that there are many who are not faithful to their partners but we usually do not expect this of a member of our own family.

When anything such as this happens within a family, each member usually feels that they not only have a right to their say and their beliefs but often expect others to come out on their side or follow the family line. Even if you believe that each person is responsible for their own lives and behaviour and that it is up to them to live their life as they wish, it is very difficult not to judge either, them, their partner or those around for the way they are behaving. This can make us feel guilty or that we have let ourselves down.

Generally we like the person whom our sibling has chosen or at the least make an effort to get on with them. In the event that we do not like them, we at least carry the expectation that if anything bad is done it will be done by them. It is therefore often a shock to discover that your sibling is having or has had an affair. It also feels that not only have they let down their partner and children but their extended family and ourselves as well.

Often we make efforts to find excuses or rationalise the situation, we look for someone else to blame. We look at the partner's behaviour and consider any of their faults. We look at our own family to see what messages we were given whilst we were growing up and carefully look to see where our parents perhaps went wrong. We look at our sibling and try to understand why. Gradually we have to accept that no matter who is at fault or who we blame, what has happened will affect the relationship we have with our sibling, their partner and other members of our family and theirs.

There are a number of ways that you might hear that this has happened, if you have heard gossip you may have tried to deny it, creating a future embarrassing situation for yourself. It is difficult to know what to say if you are told by their partner, do you believe what they are saying, defend or attack your sibling? Whose side are you on? Although you may know that what has happened is nothing to do with you, there are often feelings of embarrassment for them as well as for your family and yourself for being connected in any way.

It may be that very few people know, it is often very difficult to know who knows. Who can you talk to? Who can you tell? Can you manage not to let anything drop or behave as though nothing is happening? There is also the question of whether you should tell, are there those who have a right to know?

It can make you feel very angry that you are having to carry all this, not knowing what the right answers are and feeling that you are walking around the edge of a volcano which is likely to blow up and hurt a lot of people. It is an indication of how unbalanced it can get when you start believing that if it does it would be your fault. It is hard not to feel that you are in some way to blame although you know that this is not so.

There is always the fear that this will lead to the break-up of this relationship. If the partner found out they may leave, there is also the possibility that this affair will last and your sibling will move in with the new person. This further deterioration of the situation creates even more difficulties in family relationships. It could mean that you and your family could lose the contact you have with your nephews and nieces and the estranged parent, it is also likely that you will have very little say in the matter.

It may be that you will be expected to welcome the new partner into your family and become friends with them. This is a very difficult thing to do, something that you may not want to do but run the risk of alienating your sibling if you do not. On the other hand you will risk losing other members of your family as well as their original family if you do.

We have a lot of joint history with our adult siblings, we may love them very much, our relationship with them is very precious and we have all the times when they may have cared for or defended us. Now that they are in this situation what do we do?

There will also be requests for help, advice and guidance from other members in the family, what should they do? What are we going to do? There are demands that we should think or do as others have done. It is very difficult to work out how we feel. We may love our sibling but not approve of what they are doing but how does that translate into what we do. Whatever we do we are likely to upset a number of people.

There is also the possibility that we have been given false information. Who is telling the truth? Are people lying or are they just telling it as they but no-one else see it? It is often very difficult to know what to do when we do not know who to trust or when we suspect that someone we have always trusted and believed is not being honest. Our wish would probably be to move as far away from the situation as possible but this is probably not possible.

It is painful to accept that you and others who you care about, have been hurt, confused and had relationships damaged or lost through the actions and choice of a sibling who you care about and love. It is even harder when they do not accept responsibility for what they have done or do not appear to care.

A sibling of an offender.

Having a serious offender in the family probably says very little about the sort of person you or any other member of your family are. Unfortunately many people do not appear to realise this and will judge everyone in the family by what they have heard or understand the family is about, from reports in the press or from gossip about one member of the family.

This often leaves families feeling that they have to make some very hard decisions about whether to stay with the one who has offended and cope with the problems this creates or reject them in the hope that it will make life easier for the rest of them.

If these kind of decisions are being made it is extremely difficult for siblings, particularly if they are young, to do anything that the rest of the family do not want. This may be keeping in touch with a brother or sister or rejecting them. If it is not what the rest of the family are doing, they will generally expect you to change to do and feel the same as them. Other members of the family may feel rejected, angry and confused if everyone does not conform and often pressure is put on to make you fall in line, giving little time and space for you to decide what it is that you think, feel and want to do.

It is also likely that as the family's views and opinions are the ones that are being heard loudest and strongest, it is not only difficult to deviate from the family line but to even realise that there may be a different view point. There is also the possibility that there are so many different ideas, thoughts and views being put forward, each person believing that they are right and that everyone should do as they say. This leads to confusion and splits both within the family and between individuals.

It is also often difficult to know what the truth is, what really happened and who to believe. The opportunities for seeing and talking with your sibling are very few and are not in private, also children are often prevented by their families, from visiting their sibling in prison.

The person you knew before is likely to be gone. You cannot be relaxed with each other whilst being watched and you have both been affected by what they have done or have been accused of doing. They have also been affected by what has happened to them since their arrest, if this is the first time they have experienced this system they may be shocked, confused, bewildered, distressed, angry or rebellious.

As the sibling of someone who has committed a serious offence or has been found guilty of doing this, many areas of your life are going to be affected. Even if you manage to distance yourself well, there is always the possibility that at any time you will be connected as the brother or sister of the person who committed that offence and the word is likely to spread. The effect is likely to be curiosity or rejection, however well it is covered by politeness or kindness.

However you choose to be connected or otherwise, you will be judged. If you choose to be connected there will be those who assume that you are to some extent either the same or in sympathy with the offence. You may be viewed as being virtuous and kind to remain connected or it may be considered that you do not have the sense to become disconnected.

If you choose to disconnect yourself, there will be those who see this as sensible but others who will judge you for abandoning a member of the family, not trusting them and standing by them.

There will be many times when you feel rather helpless and lacking in hope for your own future. There will be many people who have turned their back on you and your family, those who do not wish to be 'contaminated'. This can be overt as in them refusing to speak or crossing the road rather than meeting you. It can be more subtle, with excuses given as to why they cannot continue their relationship with you in the way that they had before, they are suddenly very busy or something.

Whilst suffering from all the feelings and emotions of bereavement, from disbelief that this is happening or that they could have done this to the anger at them for what they have done to you and your family, there is often very little support or sympathy. Dealing with what is happening will take up all available time and space, though they are not there but in custody, they are very much a part of life and it feels at times that they are all there is.

Very often siblings get the backlash, parents and others thinking that because this has happened with one child, they must make sure that it will not happen again. Whether or not you are likely to offend yourself, discipline becomes heavier, freedoms are curtailed and you are watched and questioned about everything.

It may be that you never had the slightest intention of doing anything wrong. You have had to look at what your brother or sisters actions have done to everyone and are doubly aware that this is not the way you are going but it feels that you are being punished anyway. Even if you can understand why this is being done, it does not make it easier to cope with, it also makes you realise that no one is seeing or hearing you.

All too often both at home and in other areas of your life, because of what has happened and because you come from the same family, you are not given the benefit of the doubt. If something goes missing, in which direction do eyes turn? If there is trouble, who is expected or suspected of being there? Protestations do not help as they are expected and proof of innocence may only be grudgingly accepted.

It is often more difficult to make friends, parents of friends will often stop them from seeing you or spending time with you, they may not want to have you in their house and they would not want their child in yours. It becomes very easy to give up and become isolated. Widening your circle of friends and making new friends who will accept you for yourself is not easy and these new friendships feel very fragile for a long time, those friends who remained faithful are very precious.

If the court case was reported in the press, so much about your family is known by so many people, in particular the things that you would not wish most people to know. Those who do not know us feel that they do and that they have a right to discuss the wrongs and the rights, the good and the bad and what should or should not have been done. It is totally forgotten that there is so much more to a family than what is brought up in court or reported. There can be very painful feelings of total raw exposure, making it difficult to know whether to go and hide or try to defend and explain.

The question most often asked is why? and a lot of time is spent trying to find the answer. Sometimes the answer is in the way that your parents treated this particular child or it may be the way that all of you were raised. Sometimes there are other reasons both within them, their life or in society, sometimes there does not appear to be any answer at all.

It may be that whilst you are doing your exploring things may be uncovered that are difficult to cope with, for example, a young person who has been abused discovers that they were not the only one and that this was also happening to other members of the family. If they had allowed the abuse to continue, believing that in this way they were preventing it happening to others in the family, it is shattering to discover that the sacrifice had not only been pointless but doing nothing has led to a brother or sister committing a serious offence.

All too often those who have done nothing wrong are punished for being related to a person who has. Their punishment is to have to stay in a society who may avoid them out of fear, or refuse to leave them alone for the profit, entertainment or titillation it gains from the contact.

CHAPTER 2

CHILDREN; NOW AND IN THE FUTURE

What our parents did to us as children,
we believe has a great effect on how we cope with life now,
yet we believe that our children are flexible
and that they will cope, whatever we put them through.

Us now, are we these children in the future?

Even the very old, who have had time to live their own lives and learn to make their own choices, are heard to give credit to or blame their parents, for the successes or failures in their lives. For some it was the happy secure childhood that they were given, which they were able to pass on to their own children or they had been taught the value of hard work which had underpinned their success. The parents of others had ruined their lives by the way they were treated or what they were made to do.

We too learned from our parents and families and we too hold them responsible, rightly or wrongly blaming them for many of our problems. When we have been badly hurt and are feeling lost, frightened and anxious, we often become a child, coping with the child in our self. This affects the way we treat and manage our own children. Whilst we are trying to deal with all that is happening to us, we may have very little left with which to help them.

It is likely that, for quite some time after a bereavement, not only are we unable to be objective and see anything clearly but also, we are probably unable or would not wish to answer the questions: Who is the adult? Who is responsible? Who is keeping things going? Who is doing the caring? Who is being responsible? We know what the answers should be, but are probably not aware or could not face the fact that they are probably not the answers we could honestly give now.

All too often, when things go badly wrong, parents are not capable of dealing with their own problems or grief and are, at least for a while, unable to support, help or cope with those of their children. Very often the other adults are also too busy dealing with their own feelings about what has happened and are not emotionally available to the children. They may in fact be totally absent, distancing themselves from the problems or wanting to avoid becoming involved, leaving no-one for the children to turn to.

Often children have to put away their own grief to cope with parents or others who are not coping. They frequently have to be the responsible adult, keeping things going, doing the caring and not showing their true feelings, to avoid causing further distress to their parents.

It is hard enough for a child to have to worry about a parent who they know is not eating or sleeping, to see their home becoming a mess and trying to clear it up or cook a meal, whilst trying to keep up with their school work. It is even harder to put a drunk parent to bed, to try to keep things safe when a parent is past being responsible and to accept that no-one has cared about what you have been doing in any part of your life for ages.

We may be aware of what is happening, supporting each other and sharing each other's grief, but the guilt we feel at what we are doing to our children is a heavy burden. All too often we have little space in which to deal with our own or our children's grief, we do not know how we should be dealing with it, what is right or wrong, good or bad.

We do not have sufficient coping strategies, contact with anyone who may be able to help and little or no support. All too often we cling to our children like a frightened toddler to its mother or we reject them because we cannot cope with both them and us. Whilst our own pain is overwhelming us, we are unable to face or cope with theirs. They, like us, are often most on their own, when they most need support.

Their grief
Our children depend on us for many things, including supplying them with information. They need to know for example, what is going on, how to cope and deal with things and what is likely to happen. It is up to us to give them the information that they need, to be honest and to help them to understand and deal with that information. This is an enormous responsibility and although we cannot hope to get it right all the time we must try.

If they are to trust us, we must be honest but it is often difficult to know what the truth is or to know what and how much information to give, often we are able to be guided by their questions and by their understanding of our answers. A child may be able to accept a simple explanation about why a parent is becoming forgetful and confused, if they are developing Alzheimer's disease but they will probably have more difficulty accepting any answers we can give to questions about the reasons for a parent leaving. It is even more difficult to know what reasons or explanations we can give, for a parent's adultery or their imprisonment for an offence such as rape.

Children suffer grief just as we do, for what they have lost. Their grief cannot be got around by pretending that nothing has happened and that all is well, we cannot expect them to be happy, carefree children, when all those around them are falling apart. They will of course know that something is seriously wrong but if they do not know what it is and do not receive the information they need, the fear of loss that they are having to deal with may be equally as great, if not greater than the loss itself.

When all those around them are falling apart, perhaps fighting and arguing, being icily polite or not speaking, is it more terrifying for them to be told what is happening and why or to be left to make up possible reasons for themselves?

Very often it is easier and less painful to deal with the fact of what is, particularly when the facts may be the only thing that is constant. The facts may be painful but there is something to be said for knowing what you are dealing with and what you are coming to terms with.

A child's understanding of the facts will grow as they grow, gradually they will understand more and more of the implications of what they have been told. Each new step in understanding may change their perspective on the situation, their attitudes and feelings towards those involved and may also renew their feelings of pain, grief and loss. These changes can continue for the rest of their life, as they pass through their own life stages.

For example, when a parent leaves to be with a different partner, there are many things to be worked through at different ages and stages. When they leave, there is the grief of the loss of the parent and the family as it was. Initially there may be a satisfactory, ongoing relationship with that parent, but the parent's interest and their contact may gradually disappear causing another loss. Half brothers or sisters from the parents present relationships, cement those relationships but may leave the child feeling like something left over from a time that would best be forgotten.

As the child grows they become aware of such matters as, whether their poor financial state or housing condition would have existed if the parent had stayed. If the parent who has left, is financially better off and can afford things like a car and holidays that the rest of the family cannot, it is hard for a child not to feel bitter towards them.

With growing maturity comes the dawning that the parent was having a sexual relationship with their new partner, whilst their parents were still together, this may cause a lot of upset, confusion, anger and disgust, again changing the child's attitude towards their parents. Later still, when they have their own boy or girl friends and have a relationship of their own, they have to deal with the insecurities that they have been left with.

Whatever the cause of the loss, a child will be aware of their lack of control over their life and what happens to them. There is a loss of trust in life and the people who are supposed to protect them from hurt and harm. There is a loss of confidence in themselves, the world and the future.

Before this happened, as adults, we believed that these things happened to other people. Before this happened, the children did not even know that these things happened. Now they know that bad things can happen and can happen to them and no one around them can prevent it happening or protect them from the hurt. Some children are able to grow, mature and learn at least that they can survive life's tragedies, some children remain defeated and others believe that they have to keep everyone at a distance and fight to protect themselves.

Whatever their age when this happens, the age of innocence has gone and this is going to have a profound affect on the rest of their life. If they are to work through their grief successfully, to learn, grow and find their balance it is the responsibility of all to help.

Our attitudes to their grief

We do not want to face the fact that children suffer a lot of pain from the losses that often we have caused, we want to believe that things do not bother them deeply and they quickly forget or get over it. We want to see them permanently happy and care-free and become impatient or even demand this of them, when they do not respond in the way we want or they do not behave in ways that make us feel good about ourselves and our parenting.

We will often try to buy their happiness and their approval of us when we know we have hurt or failed them and when we cannot or are not willing to give them our time and attention. This is often done by parents who have left their families, they give big presents and treats to their children instead of making a relationship with them, hoping to gain and keep their child's love and approval.

When a great loss has happened to us, we know that for some time we are being a less than adequate parent. We do not want to believe that what is happening to us is also happening to our children, affecting their lives and causing them the same pain that we are suffering. Even more, we do not want to accept the fact that this is going to affect the rest of their lives, how they feel about us, themselves, the family and society.

Whether what is happening is caused by a parent, such as a parent deserting or whether it is happening to a parent, such as the development of Alzheimer's disease. Whether it is something that is happening to the child, such as becoming aware of being homosexual or something done by the child, such as a serious offence, we generally feel guilty and that we have failed them. Often to escape from the pain of this, we try to find someone or something else to blame instead of finding the cause, rarely accepting that blame is no more relevant or helpful than guilt.

When a child does something bad and we know or like the parents, we blame the child, school or society. If we do not know or like the parents we blame them. If it is our child, depending on how we feel about ourselves, we blame ourselves or our partner, school or society for not providing what was needed to prevent this happening.

We go around demanding why? why? why? but are usually very careful to avoid being in a position to really hear the answer. We rarely sit down with the child and give them the time and understanding to work out why, because there is a big chance that we would not like or be able to accept the answer.

We look around at other children and think that surely bad things must be happening to a lot of them and they appear to be fine. Look at all the children who come from one parent families that are fine, so are many that have coped with other kinds of big problems and come out of it OK. We want to believe that children are flexible and can cope.

We also believe that, as my children have got me as their parent, they really should not have too much of a problem, I love and care for them and really bad things do not happen to people like us, it will all turn out right in the end. We tell ourselves that they have to grow up sometime and see the world the way it is and that this is just a bit earlier and more sudden than we had intended.

If children have to become carers of a parent, it is often felt that it will make them grow up a little more quickly and teach them responsibility and caring. We would prefer to forget that a child becoming the carer of a parent can create many emotional problems for the child and problems for the parent, that the child has to cope with.

For these children, their experience of life is not the same as that of other children, therefore their development cannot be the same, neither can their view of themselves and of life in general. Their ability to fit in with their peers and the rest of society will not be as easy or the same as for others. They often have to provide security for themselves and the parent, before they are really able to, thereby creating difficulties in being an adult, when they have not learned to be a child and an adolescent first.

Settling down

Perhaps one of the greatest needs the child has is for security. A time to learn to feel safe again after what has happened. This can take a long time but all too often, hardly before they have begun to settle down, something else happens over which they have no say, choice or control.

There is often a chain of events such as, a brother or sister is born with a disability, later a parent leaves and the parents decide who the children are to live with. One or both parents may get new partners and sometimes these relationships break up as well, causing the child further enormous pain and distress. It is likely that there will be a house move and possibly a move to a new area, leaving everything they knew behind.

With all these changes and whilst you are trying to cope yourself, you are supposed to be making your children feel secure. To even try to do this is difficult, often we feel resentful having to provide the security that someone else took away. Often we do not have the time or the energy to cope with all the insecurities in our children, the constant requests for reassurance or their testing out of us to see if we too will let them down.

Their grief is a severe punishment, if we have not caused this grief we may feel resentful at what we are having to deal with and resent the fact that we may not have anyone to help us repair our own sense of security. We feel guilty for being any part of the cause of our children's pain and we feel that we are unable to help them sufficiently, particularly if we do not feel that we have sufficient strength and security within ourselves.

It is necessary to put at least part of our own lives aside, so that we have the space to give them the help and support they need but how much life do we have. At times it feels that there is no space to be found. It is important to have a life of our own and to have time to ourselves if we are to continue to cope. To be a good role model we have to show that though we are hurt we can pick ourselves up, start again and build a worthwhile life for ourself.

Our children need our love, the unconditional love that sometimes says 'I love you but I do not like the way you are behaving', or 'I love you and care about you but I also care about myself'. Our children will one day, want to leave, we must love them enough to let them go freely. We should have put in place a life that we have built for ourselves.

They also need understanding but not the understanding that allows just anything to be acceptable because of the bad things that have happened. All too often people say, 'I know they should not do that but ...' unacceptable behaviour is just that, unacceptable. Understanding enables us to appreciate why the behaviour happened, to see how difficult it is for the child and gives us knowledge and patience to help them.

Life goes on and so do our efforts to make a life that we all can live with. How long does it take? It takes as long as it takes. There may be many times when it feels that you are beginning to get somewhere, only to discover that this is not so.

Often the efforts children make to be OK, crack under the strains of their everyday life. Such things as the comments from other children or teachers, lack of money, or the things other children have, cause problems that appear to be totally out of all proportion. For any child, trying to be like everyone else when they feel very different can make being part of a peer group very difficult, if not impossible and in consequence desperately unhappy.

Often a child who is being very good, is doing this because they are afraid to be otherwise. Afraid to upset a parent in case they leave or go away completely. Afraid to cause more stress to an already over stressed parent, in case it causes them to break down completely. It is often hard to accept that children believe that they are responsible for what has happened and therefore often fear that they are going to be punished, the fear is also that the punishment may be further loss.

If a parent accepts responsibility for things that are not their fault, the child will often accepts that this is so and will also blame the parent. Whatever the parent is responsible for or believes they are responsible for, will often be used to beat them with. It is important that parents only accept blame for the things that they have done. If parents accept the blame for what others have done or all the ills that befall their children, the children can avoid taking responsibility for their own lives for the rest of their lives because they have their parents to blame.

Children can use the bad things that happen to them as a peg to hang all their problems on. Having a disabled sibling or a parent who has left them, can be used as the cause of all their problems, they may receive a lot of sympathy but no help to deal with life. If they are allowed do this they will not learn that, in most ways they are no different from anyone else and that people with apparently perfect lives also have problems which they have to overcome.

This behaviour can lead to the real cause of the problem being missed and therefore not dealt with. They may even hold on to what has happened and keep it as a problem, fearing that if they give it up they will not have an excuse anymore and also people will stop taking notice of them, being kind and giving them the attention they feel they need.

Any big problem can give an unbalanced picture of what is normal. For example, a child with a single parent will probably find their parent and their home embarrassing. It is often difficult for the child to accept that it is the most normal thing in the world to find your parents and home embarrassing. They would probably feel like this and have difficulties bringing friends home whatever their circumstances.

Our children are not us

The more we understand ourselves, the more we can help our children. It is important to separate ourselves and our feelings from theirs, to clearly see their feelings and problems so that we are able to help them. Our answers and our way of dealing with problems may be right for us but not necessarily right for them. It is important that we support them in finding the answers, that are right for them. How much input we have, will depend on the age and understanding of the child.

Our children do not necessarily need the same things as we did or we do now, they think their own thoughts and have their own views and opinions. We should not expect them to hate or be angry with someone just because we are. It can be extremely painful and difficult for us, to find that they like and want to spend time with someone we hate or that they have a relationship with someone that we are excluded from. We have to be careful that we do not allow our feelings about the other person or the situation to be taken out on our child.

When there is a bereavement in the family, the children's loss is in many ways different to those of the parents. For example, if a parent leaves, the relationship that the couple had has gone, but for the child, the relationship may be different but not lost. A child may be forced to choose between their parents, a parent does not have to divide their loyalties in this way. A child was not responsible for choosing the parent who has hurt them, the parents were responsible for choosing each other. The loss of a parent's love is irreplaceable, but parents may find love in a new partner.

If a parent develops Alzheimer's disease, the child loses a parent and their parent loses a partner. The child has lost the person who gave them unconditional love, who taught them, cared for them and were always there for them. Now the roles have been reversed. The partner of the one with the disease has lost a friend and companion and an equal to share things with.

As we have lived longer, we have had the opportunity to learn a lot about life, to learn some coping strategies and are less surprised at what life holds for us. Not only are children very vulnerable they have not had the time or the opportunity to learn as much about life as an adult has. If it is the first time that anything like this has happened to us, we realise how little any of our earlier experiences have equipped us to cope. How much worse then is it for a child?

We have had many experiences and have made mistakes, which we have learned from, perhaps we have changed our ways or will not make the same mistake again. However hard we try, our children will rarely learn from the mistakes we have made, they are far more likely to learn from their own experiences. They have their own lessons to learn and their own lives to live.

In our hearts we know how we want our children to be, we want to be proud of them. We may want them to be like us or different, depending on how we feel about ourselves. Through them we try to put right the things that we feel were wrong in our lives and expect them to appreciate our efforts. We want them to learn from us even though we refused to learn from our parents. We wanted to protect them from pain and hurt but with this happening, we realise that this is something we cannot do.

Providing for some of their needs

It is impossible to know what effect things, will have on a child's life and their future but we do know that those involved in their care can make a big and positive difference to the outcome, if they provide support, care, encouragement and stability. A lot of effort must be made to provide positive experiences, which not only counter-balance the negative ones, but also fill in the gaps in their experience. For example, a child without a father will need good male role models, children without a mother, good female ones. These can be provided by many people, in many different ways and settings.

Parents who split up, should both maintain a good relationship with their children, care about them and be there for them. It is important that the contact is maintained, even though this may have to be infrequent, quality being far more important that quantity. It is important that the child believes that they are of value and worth holding on to.

The break-up of their parent's relationship is devastating to a child, even if the relationship was not good. The break-up of a parent's second relationship, particularly where the child has developed a good relationship with the new partner, can cause distress that many children never completely recover from. It can often cause problems in their own relationships and in other areas of their life, their mental health may also suffer for the rest of their life.

All too often parents rush into a new relationship, before they have themselves come to terms with what has happened, before the family has time to get used to its loss of membership and before the children have had time to begin to grasp what has happened. The parent chooses their new partner and brings them into the home but the children have no say or control over whether this new person enters not only their home but all areas of their life. The new partner probably has a say in all things including bedtime, how and when things are done and what time is curfew. We often hear how hard it is to be a step-parent and this is true but how often do we consider, how hard is it to be a step-child?

179

Very often the things that happen involve the sexuality and sexual behaviour of parents, even more often this is the element that is avoided, not explained and often denied. As the child grows older, they not only have the distress of realising what their parents have done but also that they lied or avoided the truth. Children are taught that doing what their parent did is wrong but when they become aware of what it is that their parent did, it is either not supposed to affect how they feel about that parent or it is supposed to make them hate the parent, depending on who they are talking to.

If the parent is disabled, creating difficulties and making life very hard, it is often supposed to make the child more tolerant, accepting and understanding. This is very difficult to do if no one is showing these qualities toward the child, it is often forgotten that these are not automatic gifts bestowed on child carers. Unless a child is shown tolerance, acceptance and understanding of themselves and their own feelings, how can they have them to show to others. Just because the person they care for is someone they love, both the child and the parent, do not turn into patient, gentle angels.

Children just like adults, need space and time to grieve, they need to have stability, support and care whilst they mourn for their losses and come to terms with what they have. They need to do this in their own time and their own way.

Many people will try to impose time limits and particular ways of behaving, for many different reasons. Some children will try to conform to these other will fight them, but if their grieving is not allowed to follow its natural and necessary course, sooner or later problems will arise for the child, the family or their future partners and possibly all of them.

Changing and adapting

Children are flexible and adaptable if they feel secure, loved and accepted. Just because they are able to adapt and cope with changes, it does not mean that it is painless. Often we unthinkingly put our children through a lot of pain and suffering because of our thoughtlessness or so that we can do whatever it is that we want to do.

Even if we do consider them and take them into account, there are times when things happen or we have to make changes that will cause our children to suffer. It is necessary that we should be truthful and protect them before considering ourselves. It is not necessarily helpful to understand our children from our own view point, we must try to understand what it is that they are seeing, what it feels like to them, what they have heard and understood and what it is that they are telling and asking us.

We must not judge them, they cannot help how and what they feel any more than we can help the way we feel. They need our help to understand themselves, their reactions, feelings and what is happening to them. It is only then, that they can begin to learn to accept themselves and their feelings, learn their own coping strategies and safe ways of expressing themselves and their feelings.

They must be allowed to feel anger, hate and hurt and be able to express them. They must also be able to own their bad feelings as well as the good ones and accept these parts of themselves, just as we must accept these parts of our child and of ourselves. If we have not or cannot accept these parts of ourselves, we will be unable to accept them in our children, then the love that we give them cannot be unconditional.

We need to admit our own feelings, at least to ourselves and if necessary find the help we need to cope. This event has happened to all of us at the same time and hurt us all but this also means that we can move forward together. We accept that our grieving will take a long time and that we will be affected, possibly for the rest of our lives, therefore it would be foolish to believe that it will have any less effect on the children. They too have to learn that however much they wish for things to be different, they must accept that things are the way they are.

As we move forward together and rebuild our lives, we should remember that if we consider our children, they will learn to consider us, if we are loyal to them they will be loyal to us. From the love and caring they receive from us, they will learn to love and care. By helping and allowing them to be who and what they are and when they have grown, freely letting them go, we both discover that from the loss we suffered, we gain a very special relationship.

CHAPTER 3

PARENTS AND GRANDPARENTS

Our children are only ours for a while,
we must let them go, to live their own lives.
But we remain connected, hurt by their hurt,
embarrassed by their mistakes, we still care.

Connections

Through birth and marriage we are connected to older and younger generations, how close we are in our lives varies from family to family and from individual to individual. Our parents are connected to us as we are to our children, as our grandparents are to our parents. Our parents are connected to our children both through us and directly with their grandchildren.

It is obvious then, that when anything bad happens to or is done by ourselves or our children, our parents are connected to the pain and loss. Also, because of their close connection, they are in a unique position to give the greatest help and support.

Whether this happens or not and how much, depends not only on how geographically close they live but mostly on how good the relationship is between them and ourselves.

It is very difficult for an outsider to know how good the relationship is and how much help and support is being given. Many people are enormously grateful for a very small amount of help others believe that it is wrong to criticise their family to someone outside the family. Therefore it is easy to assume that someone is receiving a lot of help and support from their parents and other members of their family, when this is not so.

It is often thought that a relationship is good, helpful and supportive because those involved spend a lot of time together and frequently include each other in their conversations, unfortunately this may be far from the reality.

Often individuals are not aware of the true state of their relationship, a lot of people believe their relationship is very different to what it is. If the relationship is not honest one can be very misled. For example, a parent may spend a lot of time helping at the home of their child, unaware that this is not appreciated or that their space would be preferred. There are a lot of people who believe they are helping but in fact, what they are doing is not helpful and the recipient is left feeling that the cost of this help to them, in time, effort and energy is very expensive.

The help that one person needs, may not be the same as another, people are often not asked what help they need, the helper just does what they feel is right. There are many who are only willing to give help on their own terms or do certain tasks. This is fine as long as the recipient is able to use the help on offer and it may be better than no help at all. There is always the risk that they will feel compelled to use the help because it is being offered and they feel unable to refuse, even though it is not useful and may in fact create more work or problems for the one who is supposedly being helped.

In some cases, parents and grandparents are able to give very little help because they live too far away or because their health is poor but they can and often do give a lot of emotional support, for many the telephone is a lifeline. For other people, their parents are a tower of strength, providing both practical and emotional support, from this kind of help, relationships grow and all the members of the family benefit.

They are still our parents

It can make the relationship very difficult if there are strict boundaries and parents still believe that they are at the top of the hierarchy, know best and expect everyone to accept this. It is important that they recognise how old we are and treat us as adults and accept that this is happening to us, this is our problem and we must deal with it. Some parents at times of stress, return to being 'parents' and either restrict our autonomy or take over our place in our own family, leading to confusion, resentment and a lot of bad feeling.

The pain and distress they are feeling together with their wish to fix it and make everything better, sometimes makes them feel that this is in fact their problem and it is happening to them. This can lead to attempts to try to take over and run everything, often taking on responsibilities that they have taken from others whether they wish it or not. Their distress may also cause them to forget that this is in fact not happening to them but to someone else, to the extent that they demand the lion's share of all the time, sympathy and attention which they believe they deserve.

It is difficult if the older generation do not respect the wishes and priorities of their children and grandchildren, who they are supposedly helping, thus creating problems and frictions. It is even more difficult when they refuse to carry out or undermine treatments or programmes which have been prescribed. Things such as giving sweets and chocolate to a child who is allergic or seriously over weight, not keeping to routines when they are caring for a child or being a bad role model, behaving badly and encouraging inappropriate behaviour from a child they are supposedly being responsible for.

They can also be very indiscreet, perhaps at a social occasion telling our colleagues about our personal problems and difficulties and how they have helped and supported us through them or by describing some of the worst excesses of our children's behaviour. They may need to talk, to share or to receive some social recognition but are perhaps unaware of the level of embarrassment and distress they are creating for everyone or that they may be ruining chances of future promotion.

Our parents wish to be proud of our successes, and us they also want to see that their efforts have been worthwhile. A bereavement, at least for a while can take all this away. Often in their effort to be positive or in their genuine awareness of the effort that has been put in, they may tell others of some of our achievements that we would prefer not to have broadcast.

If we have not told others that we have been depressed, we may not be too delighted if a parent tells everyone about our brave and successful fight against it. If our child is gay, just coming to terms with this and no-one outside the immediate family knows, they probably do not need an open minded grandparent telling everyone that they meet how well the young person and the family are coping with this.

It is often difficult for parents who have always helped, supported and been closely involved with their children to feel outside what is happening, to allow the children and their family to deal with it and only help when it is required or asked for. It is painful for them to see their children and grandchildren suffering, it makes them feel helpless not to be able to make everything better.

As they get older, the amount of help they are able to give also becomes less and they have to cope not only with their feelings and fears about their own failing abilities and their own mortality. Also they realise that they may stop being able to help and could become a burden to their children, who already have more than enough to cope with.

What can they offer?

One of the main things that parents and grandparents can offer and bring to any situation, are greater maturity and a wider or at least longer experience of life. They have raised their own children and grandparents have had a hand in helping with the next generation.

They have often seen how many problems that once appeared enormous, resolve themselves or just disappear with the passing of time. They have seen things that were great scandals at one time disappear, to be remembered by no-one a few years later, they also remember how their own heartaches were eased and ways of coping were found as time passed.

If they have learned from their experiences, they will have gained knowledge and understanding of not only how to help but what is helpful. How to bring some calmness to a fraught situation, to have some idea when an adult child needs their inner child to be comforted and when they need the encouragement of trust in their ability to cope alone.

Many older people will have time to help, time to listen and time just to be. It is a special gift if they are able to be there for whoever in the family needs them. Very often this is particularly important for the younger generation, for them to have someone who has the time and space to be there whilst they try to work out what it is all about, how to cope and where they fit in.

Parents dealing with their child with special needs or one who has committed an offence or coping with a confused relative, are left with very little time or energy for the rest of the family. Parents need the help and support of the older generation that they can trust to help the younger generation.

To the others in the family, a grandparent who is willing to give some time and understanding is a precious gift, enabling them to feel secure and cared about. The grandparent can help them to better understand and cope with their difficult feelings, help them to see the wider picture and have a better understanding of the individuals involved, what they are feeling and why they are behaving in the way that they are.

Grandparents and their grandchildren are often able to develop a very strong bond, enabling a child to have a special someone to go to when they feel that their parents are unable to cope or help. This also gives the older person a special role and place within the family which is all too often missing in our society.

Where is the life after children?

Very often, where there is a bereavement without a death, it is not a matter of filling up the space that has been left but giving up the space that we had hoped to fill with other things. For those who are older, with children who have grown up and leading their own lives, they are able to come and go as they want and look forward to retirement when the world can become their oyster and clock watching a thing of the past. Suddenly something has happened which has taken much of the peace and freedom away.

If a grandchild has special needs, so much more is needed than a little regular babysitting and in other situations much of life can be spent transporting, caring, listening and often filling in for the adult who is not there either out of choice or from necessity.

It may be that after a child's marriage fails they will need to return home to live, many will now have children and even if the children are not there full time they may stay for regular weekend visits. The peace and quiet are gone; the ornaments are at risk and the general chaos of childhood returns. Many parents willingly take this on and help to deal with all the difficulties and problems, often not considering the long-term implications or their own losses.

For a short while this may be all right but it is a different matter when it is for a long time. Some situations will resolve themselves after a while when life has settled down into a new order but there is also the possibility that the losses of the new order will bring their own losses.

For example, a parent may be very happy to have their child and grandchildren living with them. If they are widowed it may even bring a sense of life, purpose and usefulness to them but then their child may leave to be with a new partner and they are again alone trying to cope with this further loss.

Many others would be glad to have their home back to themselves and have a more quiet and peaceful life. In some situations the loss of the life that was planned for and expected is very hard to accept, replacing the time to enjoy yourself and please yourself, with the role of carer and supporter. It may be that you are not the main carer but it is hard to go away and enjoy your own time when the lack of your help means that someone who will not get a break has to work even harder in your absence.

Often the feelings of resentment are overwhelming as you see your friends free and getting on with their lives, to see them not having to share a home that was the right size for one or two being taken over by a family. There are the feelings of embarrassment and failure if your child's marriage has failed or you have a child or grandchild who has committed a serious offence. You wonder where you went wrong.

Sometimes the boundaries become confused, this may be a natural consequence if a grandparent cares for the child of a single parent and takes over the role of surrogate parent. Sometimes it is the parents who hand over the care of their children to the grandparents, so that they can have the sort of life they want as unencumbered by children as possible. At other times it is the grandparents who take over, this may or may not be what the parents want. If it is not, then it can cause a lot of anger and resentment particularly in situations where it is necessary for them to rely on the parents or grandparents help.

It can create confusion and anxiety in the children, if they are not clear which people are their parents and which ones are their grandparents. It can be difficult to know whose instructions to follow and who to go to if there is a problem, they know in this situation that whoever they choose there is likely to be trouble. Sometimes they have to listen to each criticising and blaming the other or each trying to get the child to love them the most, making the child feel torn in two. If they feel the people they love tearing them apart, it is almost guaranteed that eventually everyone will lose.

There are those parents and grandparents who do not give much help and support, some of these are in fact fairly dependant themselves, expecting care and support whilst giving very little back. This can make life difficult enough, but it is even worse that some of these relatives appear to the rest of society as wonderful, kind and helpful people. It is galling to be regularly told what a wonderful person they are, how lucky you are to have them. Their perceived virtues are extolled, when in fact none of these fit or are demonstrated in your situation but this is how they appear to other people.

There are those whose help is minimal, sometimes this is through ill health but often it is because they cannot face the reality of the situation. If they are not willing or able to face and work through their own grief, are denying what has happened or that there is a problem, they may retreat into their own problems and difficulties, whether real or imaginary and are unable or unwilling to see or go any further.

There are many parents and grandparents who are very unsupported, they have no one to turn to themselves, no one to talk to or lean on but they are expected to be able to continually give support and help. Society expects them to care and cope but rarely looks at their needs. Perhaps because this is not happening directly to them, their needs are not considered. Presumably they are expected to just walk away if it gets too difficult or because they are parents or grandparents they are just expected to cope. It is very important that they and others respect the amount of time and energy they have, allow them to have a life of their own and to live it.

A special needs child

The birth of a grandchild is a very important event, if the child is born with a significant learning disability it is devastating. Reactions can vary from total rejection, anger and the belief that it must be the fault of the in-law family, "there is nothing like this in our family" to immediate acceptance and commitment to do whatever is needed. There are times when a parent has not initially been able to accept their special needs child and the grandparents have stepped in and cared for the children, until the parents have regained their balance.

Grandparents need time to grieve and come to terms with what has happened. Many of their losses are the same as those of the parents, such as the loss of the expected child and all that means to them. They also have to cope with watching the pain and distress of their own child. People often feel that it would be easier to cope if this was happening to them, rather than have to watch helplessly whilst someone they love is suffering.

Although this has happened to the baby, in many cases it is not the child who suffers but the parents, grandparents and those who care.

After a special needs child is born, there often has to be a lot of re-thinking about the future care of the child. If the mother had plans to return to work after the birth, she may decide that care outside the family is not possible or desirable now, so often she has to give up working to be the one to care for the child. In some families the decision may be made for a grandparent to give up working, to care for the child instead.

Whatever the level of help and support that is given, if the generations work together, the help that the grandparents give can often prevent the parents becoming exhausted and it may be that their help and support can prevent the breakdown of the parents' marriage.

The main problem is, that the problem does not go away. If it does it usually means the death of the child, which in most cases is a totally unacceptable answer. For some families the child may live for many years under the threat of death, this is a painful and difficult thing for their families to live with. But in most cases the child will live to adulthood and require continuous care and attention for many years, often requiring parents and grandparents to care for the rest of their active lives.

Often the grandparents feel that they do not have the necessary energy to deal with a young energetic child or the strength to lift and carry an older one. Sadly, as the child grows, the needs and problems change but the requirement of energy from carers and the need for their help does not go. There are often more services provided for children than for adults with special needs, so as the need for family support changes and may become greater, those who are giving the care become older, less energetic and are gradually able to give less and less help.

Grandparents also come to the point of requiring some care and attention themselves, the same care and attention that they gave their parents and hoped they would receive themselves when their time came. Now it is obvious that this is not to be, they are not going to have the opportunity to sit back and relax, because if they do, they are aware that they may be over-stretching those they are supposed to be helping.

A gay grandchild

Grandparents may be young or old, informed or uninformed, they have the same prejudices as anyone else and if they are told that a grandchild is gay, they may or may not find this extremely difficult to deal with.

Attitudes to homosexuality have changed a lot in the past few years, an older person may find it difficult to change the attitudes that they were brought up with and that were the accepted way of thinking in their youth. It is also a fact that prejudice against those who are homosexual is still held by many young people now, after all it is not the aged who go out 'gay bashing'.

Not only is there the attitude that homosexuality is disgusting but due to lack of publicity and awareness in the past, many older people feel that this is a modern phenomenon and that it only happened to an occasional person in their day. Such people were not only punished by being put in prison but were totally ostracised by everyone. It was difficult for family members to admit that they still had contact (perhaps a good reason for keeping it quiet).

There still remains a belief that this is a passing phase, an attention getting exercise, something that should or can be treated or that it will be sorted out by a good marriage. Therefore if grandparents are told, they will often refuse to accept what this really means and the long- term implications. They will often be impatient with their grandchild who they believe is not doing what they should to put the situation right.

There are grandparents who will be fully aware of the situation and all the implications, many of these will be there for all the members of the family and will be able to listen and give support. Many grandparents will have known of other gay people who have had successful and happy lives as well as the tragedy that has all too often been the lot of those whose sexual orientation is different to the norm, giving the grandparents an open and accepting attitude.

Being one generation removed it is not their child, grandparents can often see the wider picture and put this aspect of their grandchild's life in perspective, seeing them as a whole person. On the other hand there are those who are unable to see beyond this situation and are unable to accept or deal with homosexuality in any situation but especially in their own family and are therefore angry, impatient and rejecting.

A serious offender

The shock of a serious offence being committed by a grandchild may be exacerbated by the attention that you are given by the press, the initial distress having to be coped with under siege. It is very difficult to have to watch everything that you say, not knowing when you are going to be quoted rightly, wrongly or out of context, whilst in a state of shock.

When your child or grandchild is found guilty of an offence, the shame and guilt can be enormous. If you believe that there has been a miscarriage of justice, you will have very few supporters and a difficult time ahead if you decide to follow this through. If they have in fact committed the offence it is difficult to know how you are going to deal with this, what if anything, does it say about you and what will it say about you to others.

If you are the parent of an adult offender who has children, help will be needed by the parent who has been left at home to care for the children. Help is needed to look after them whilst the parent has a break, to go out to work, or to visit their partner in prison. Grandparents of a young offender, may need to give help and support to their siblings when the parent is stressed or is unable to be objective or to see things from the child's viewpoint. All the family will need time, care and support. The help that is needed will depend on the age, position in the family and the responsibilities and difficulties that they are having to cope with.

It may be that even though you are their grandparent, you may feel that you cannot have anything further to do with them or their family because of what they have done, the life that they have been living and will probably continue to live, unless they can convince you that they have changed their ways for good.

Very few people will be able to give up a child or grandchild without a second's thought, usually this is only done in either extreme circumstances or where the beliefs that are held, do not allow any other decision to be made. The soul searching can be crippling and the decision may only be made by refusing to consider feelings and emotions and only dealing in 'logic' or beliefs.

It can be very hard to allow others, particularly other members of the family, to choose to do what they wish. In some families, those who have not done what they have been told or what everyone else is doing are also rejected, causing friction and often deep divisions within the family.

Some grandparents blame their own child or the person who their child married for the problems that have happened, often accusing them of many things such as being bad parents or spoiling their children. For some people it feels very much harder to lose a grandchild than it does a child particularly if the relationship had broken down between grandparents and parents, the children being the link and hope for the future.

It is also a fact that you may be responsible for what your children have done, you are not responsible for their children, they are. It may be that the grandparent will keep contact with the offender but will reject their own child or perhaps give their own child a very hard time. Never letting them off the hook for a moment, never letting them forget that their parent believes that they have failed both as a child and a parent.

A marriage break-up through adultery

Again this is a situation which leaves parents and grandparents feeling embarrassed, hurt, confused and believing to some extent that they have failed as parents. Even if they did not like the partner, they did not wish to see this happening and the relationship end like this. It is hard to have to admit that it is their child or grandchild who has caused all this hurt and grief.

For many people, when marriages break up in this way it means that they are going to lose contact with the partner of their child. If they liked and loved this person, it is a great loss. In some situations the one who has gone was their child or grandchild who then has given up all contact with their family and have left their partner and children as the ones still in contact and receiving help from their parents.

However things divide up, so much has been lost. For parents and grandparents it is the people that they have got to know who will be lost or the relationship that they had with them. Sometimes it is contact with the grandchildren that they have lost, the grandparents being prevented from having contact with them. Even if the relationship between two people has been totally destroyed, it is very sad when the children and their grandparents are punished by being prevented from seeing or even speaking to each other.

There are times when it can become so bad, that children are prevented from speaking to their grandparents if they meet in the street. Even if they are heartbroken and cannot accept this, there is little that grandparents can do, although there may be some redress through the courts.

It is hard for a partner who has been deserted to maintain a good relationship with their in-laws. Sometimes to achieve this, it is necessary for the parents of the partner who has gone to completely reject their own child. In other situations if the relationship was good, a new but different one can be built if all concerned can reach out, work together and ignore the unhelpful or damaging comments made by others.

As well as coping with the break-up of the relationship and the loss to you of their partner, it may be that you are expected to welcome the new partner into the family. This is something that some parents and grandparents find they are unable to do, particularly if they feel that this is the person who broke up the family and without whom all this loss and grief would not have happened.

Very often when a marriage breaks down, one of the partners will return home bringing their children with them. For many grandparents, though they may love their grandchildren dearly, living with them is another matter. To allow their child to work, grandparents also often become unpaid carers, giving up their freedom and retirement as well as peace and quiet. It is the grandparents here who long for the end of the holidays and for school to resume.

It is important for grandparents to remain balanced and remember that the children's parents are still their parents, even if they are totally absent and whatever their own views are of them. It is very hard to watch the children's pain and suffering caused by a parent who is still adored by the child and to keep your own views, thoughts and feelings to yourself.

Many grandparents will be aware that at the end of the day children grow up and make their own judgement of their parents whatever direction someone has tried to push them in. If you push, you will also be judged. For a while at least, children will hang on to and love a bad or absent parent and the picture they paint may be very rosy but eventually time and reality will paint its own picture.

CHAPTER 4

RELATIVES, FRIENDS AND NEIGHBOURS

If the relatives we have, are given to us by chance,
our neighbours are chosen by what we can afford
and our friends are chosen from those we meet,
can we always have those we need and deserve?

When bad things happen to us, they can change the way we think and feel about things, the way we run our lives, the things we do, the friends we have and the relationships we have with people. We may experience a total shake-up in our lives, which may go on for some time but the effects of it may be felt for the rest of our lives. Friends may leave our lives whilst others enter it, we may move house and have new neighbours, we may move further away from or deepen the relationships we have with our relatives.

Often all of this is going on whilst we are trying to cope with our losses. It is therefore hardly surprising that we often do not do things well and that some of the relationships that we had and some that we make at this time go badly wrong. It is sometimes more surprising, that coping with difficulties can cement us together for life.

The nature of the problem affects the responses

The nature of the problems and how they impinge on other people affects their attitude, willingness to help, the support they give or their efforts to distance themselves as much as possible. For example, there is an enormous difference between the help and support that is needed to care for a learning disabled child who is quiet, easy going, happy and co-operative and one who is strong, aggressive and violent. The parents of both these young people need a break but although the latter may need help, much more than the former, unsurprisingly if there is any help on offer, it will rarely be for the one most in need.

Neighbours need their sleep but so do parents, it is very difficult for both parents and neighbours of a child who screams and cries most of the night. Each may feel for the other and try to appreciate their problems and difficulties but they each have their own needs and are unable to do anything about the situation.

Both parties are struggling with feelings of guilt, anger and frustration. Whilst feeling exhausted, each household has to cope with the moans and complaints of all who are home, about being kept awake and expressions of concern about coping with school or work the next day. It is unlikely that these neighbours will offer help, they are likely to feel that they have done more than their share by not becoming abusive.

Everything is also affected by where people are coming from, their own experiences and how these have effected them, their prejudices and beliefs, how emotionally stable they are and what is going on in their lives at the moment. Very often problems arise because of what is going on in the lives and minds of those around us. If someone is coping well with difficult problems it makes others feel inadequate. Some people feel that it is up to each family to cope with their own problems and would therefore not feel that it is up to them to help with what they see as someone else's problems.

There are those who feel uncomfortable around those with problems when they have not really got any themselves. Instead of at least appreciating their good fortune, they often explain at length how and why their life is not really as good as it looks and often insist that the other person's problems are not really as big or unusual as they think.

It may be surprising to realise that there are those who are jealous of people who have problems and the attention that they are getting. This can be shown in a number of different ways. They may tell the parents of a child with special needs how lucky they are that their child is not more disabled. It may be pointed out that they are getting allowances for this, their child gets taxis to school and at least they will never have a problem with their child being on drugs or getting drunk.

Those who are married may point out to someone who has been deserted how lucky they are not to have a partner to put up with or the parent of a gay child may be told that at least they are not going to have to cope with an illegitimate grandchild. They may develop problems of their own which they talk about at length or they may claim to have given a lot of help and support which they have not, so that they can claim to be part of the situation. If you feel that this notion is rather unkind or fanciful, so initially was the idea of Munchausen syndrome by proxy.

Some everyday problems

Many people find it is difficult to know what to do or say to someone who has been bereaved. There are very few, if any definite right answers but there are a number of wrong ones. Reassuring someone rarely helps, nor do long stories about your problems or those of everyone else even where they are similar and meant to reassure or show you understand.

It is also irritating, hurtful and belittling to be told that there are others worse off than you, we already know this, someone else having troubles is unlikely to make ours go away or feel better. Being made to feel bad in whatever way about someone else, does not relieve our stress but tends to make it worse. However if someone truly cares and is concerned about us, this is what will show and be felt, even if the words that are spoken are not quite right.

There is often the fear that what you do or say will be misinterpreted, it is even difficult to know whether to look or look away when we see someone who is different. I once naively believed there might be an answer and in a group for parents of children with severe learning disabilities we discussed this problem. One parent liked people to look at her and smile, if they looked away she felt rejected and felt that people could not bear to look at her child. Another parent said if people looked at her she felt she was being stared at because her child was a freak, if people smiled she felt that they were laughing at her.

One felt that it was good if people spoke to her, if they asked questions she could use this opportunity to inform and educate others, another felt that if people spoke they were being nosy and she told them where to go. If people offered to help, one parent thought that this was a criticism and that they were saying that she was inadequate and could not cope, another felt that if no-one offered to help she was either invisible or that no-one cared.

Being unsure of what is the best thing to do, is probably in fact the best way forward. How can any of us know what another wants or needs, there are many who are all too ready to impose their thoughts and views on others whether they are wanted, helpful, relevant or not. So many people are amazingly grateful for a smile, a kind word and a little help from another person, it would be very sad not to make the effort just because we were afraid that we might get it wrong, if we are unsure we can always ask.

Just as there are those who cannot ask for or accept help, there are those who feel unable to offer help, in case they are stuck with more than they wanted or will be able to cope with. Of course this can happen, particularly if you are not clear about what or how much you are offering or if you offer more than you can give or sustain. There is no point offering more than you can give, you will only end up unable to give anything. It is true that there are those who will take advantage and it is often difficult to say no, but it is worthwhile remembering that it is only possible to be taken advantage of if you allow it.

Problems for special occasions

Special occasions can be a bit of a headache at the best of times, if we want everything to be perfect we immediately hit a problem if there are going to be people there. To begin to deal with this we generally start with who will we invite, some are left trying to think of enough people whilst others need to cut down their list. Whichever way it is, there are always those we do not want to invite and all too often they are attached to someone we do.

For the relatives, friends and neighbours of those who have been bereaved and are still not totally 'recovered' there is immediately a problem. Is this person going to be miserable? Are they going to talk about their problem all evening? Are they going to discuss the politics, government attitude or local provision for those suffering from the problem? This may cause enough discomfort all round if the problem is something like Down's Syndrome but it could be much more difficult if it is something like Gay Rights, the rights of single parents or child support.

Some problems can be side stepped such as not inviting any children to an occasion such as a wedding because they may become bored and disruptive but what is to be done about an adult with a learning disability. It may be that there are those who would not come to a party if they knew that other guests may be gay. The newly separated can create the problems of the host not knowing whose side any of the other guests are on and how is the partner of a serious offender to be introduced. So very often such problems are dealt with by 'the difficulty' not being invited.

This all highlights the fact that we can easily become our problems, we become an extension of our suffering and grief at what has happened to someone close to us or what they have done. We become totally identified with our loss, sometimes not in our own eyes but in the eyes of others and their avoidance feels very much the same as rejection.

One of the great things that others can do for us is to make sure that they and others continue to see us as the people we are, separate from our situation and what is happening to us, keeping this to the fore, particularly at those times when we lose it ourselves. If we do not have a job or a career, or work mates and colleagues who see us in our work role and recognise us as one of them, part of their life and workplace, it is even more difficult to separate ourselves from our problems and the problems of those around us.

Meeting new people

What and how much to say about our losses when we meet new people is a continuing and permanent problem. How big a problem it is depends on a number of things, such as who it is that we are meeting, where we are meeting, how we feel about what has happened and how we feel we will be judged. The decision has to be made whether to say anything about what has happened or not. If you do not will anyone else say anything? If so will this be better or worse, or will your silence on the matter create a problem later?

There are often opportunities to meet new people, but for many people where there has been a bereavement, there will also be a house move, often to a different area where perhaps everyone will be new. A close relative of a serious offender may move to a new area where they are not known. The family of a child with special needs may move to be nearer a school that better meets the needs of their child. A divorced person may move to make a new start or because they can no longer afford the house they were living in and a couple who have decided to make a fresh start after an affair often begin with a new house in a new town.

The relatives of a serious offender have the difficult problem of potentially being unacceptable or of novelty value if people find out who they are. For them it usually seems best to let as few people know as possible but there is always the problem that when and if people do find out they may feel hurt that they were not trusted or will feel that they have been deceived into believing your life was something it is not.

The parents of the special needs child are attached to their child and to the new school and often the fact that there are differences is obvious. On the occasions when they are not out with their child, telling people they meet can save a lot of embarrassment later but it also has the disadvantage of perhaps either making the other person uncomfortable or the conversation may, yet again, become dominated by the subject of special needs.

A divorcee may not like to admit to their status as they would prefer those who might make unwelcome advances to believe that they were married but they might wish for those who they would like to know much better, to know that they are single. To be a single parent means that there may be certain judgements made about you and prejudices against you, there will also be certain expectations of your children, such as their abilities and behaviour and it may be necessary for you and them to climb over these.

If you are trying to recover from your partner's affair and have moved with them to make a new start, it may be that you have never had the opportunity to talk about the grief you have suffered to anyone or received any sympathy, support or understanding. Sometimes the need to talk becomes very strong and in a place where you do not know anyone very well there is the advantage of it being easier to talk to a comparative stranger. However this can create the problem of not knowing what your friendship will be in the future. Will you want a friend to know about this or if this person does not become your friend what might they do with this information in the future.

New friends and support groups
Very often we meet many of our new friends through what has happened. Through telling someone and finding that there is a connection, through other parents, support groups, in waiting rooms and by becoming friends with those we first meet as helpers. Friends and relatives also often introduce us to other people who are dealing with some of the same problems and who also become our friends.

The main disadvantage of this is that it is very easy to become totally absorbed in the problem, all our friends and life are built around it and we lose contact with anyone or anything else. Sometimes this happens because you are or feel rejected by society but very often because you do not have the time or energy to get away from it and there is no-one to help you out.

This is particularly so in the case of carers. They spend most time caring for the one in their care, some time is spent on necessary chores, with others who need their help and support, at school or hospital, with support groups and with others in the same situation for mutual help and cheering up. What time and energy is left? Time to fundraise, time to lobby, time to do all the jobs that have not been done.

The main advantage of having friends in similar situations is that they understand. They understand the full extent of what I am saying when I say anything. For example, when I told them my son had peeled potatoes, they knew, that they looked more gouged than peeled, that this had taken weeks to achieve, hours of patient teaching, bravery in allowing him to use a peeler and enormous amounts of effort and patience by him.

They know this is something to celebrate, but that there is also the underlying sadness that this should be such a cause for celebration, they know the sense of elation at the success and the dread at the thought of the effort the future is going to need.

Friends with similar problems not only have more idea how we feel but also know many of the problems we face and have to deal with. These problems may be coping with an ex-partner and access visits, it may be the feelings that we have about prison visiting, it may be the difficulty we have coping with the reactions of those we meet. They may have found coping strategies that we can share, they may be able to help us find our own, they may have worked out different ways of looking at things or point us in the direction of help we did not know about. As we move on we also can offer to others what we have learned and gained.

There is a lot to be gained from being part of a group or organisation that deals with our particular problem. Here we will meet many people who are going through the same things that we are, there will be those who are further ahead and can help us to avoid certain difficulties, give advice on what to do and encourage us, if only by the fact that they have survived. We can play our part by offering the same to others, supporting when we can and being supported when we can't.

It is very important to remember that not all those with the same problem are the same. If one person is very rich and another is very poor, it is possible and probably even likely that their experiences will be very different. It is a very different experience for example, bringing up a child with a learning disability single handed and on benefits to bringing them up with the help of a nanny and the ability to afford what is wanted as well as having holidays and breaks.

Even where there is a shortage of services, they are available to those who have the money to buy them privately. Whether this is therapy for a child, suitable accommodation for a confused relative or legal representation for someone appearing in court. Money cannot change what has happened or take away a lot of the pain but it can make a great difference not only to how we cope but also to the outcome.

It is also a different experience for someone who has a large, loving, caring and supportive family than it is for someone who is alone and for whom there is no love or support available. It is highly likely that in all these situations, whether they realise it or not, each party will have very little understanding of the other's situation and what they are going through.

There are some people who would never be friends no matter what their situation is and whatever has happened to them, there are others whose situation appears to be completely different but they become great friends. The connection is often not the particular problem but more a matter of money, lifestyle, personality or family background.

It can be very difficult and damaging to self-confidence, to find that you do not fit into a particular group where you expected to find friends, to find that you do not feel comfortable or are not getting any help or support. In fact it can make you feel even more isolated to feel alone in this situation. If this is the case do not give up, it is probably a matter that you have not found the right group for you. There are people somewhere else with whom you will feel comfortable and at ease, where you feel at the very least that those around you understand.

Friends and relatives and relatives as friends

To our relatives we have an automatic connection, this also brings the bad things that happen to each of us closer. This connection should also give all in the family, links to support and care. Unfortunately this is not always the case, there are many families where even close members are not caring and supportive, where each member is left to cope with whatever problems they have on their own.

There is also the other side of the coin, relatives have less choice in whether they give help or not, there is a built in sense of duty which makes it very difficult to avoid helping when asked. Many people feel that they do not have a right to say no to any request for help from a family member, regardless of the cost to themselves.

Often the best friendship and support comes from relatives who have become friends, the common background and shared experiences, together with the family connections and commitment gives strength and depth to the relationship. If there are problems and difficulties it is far harder to walk away if you are related, because it is difficult to move completely out of each others lives, this makes it more likely that efforts will be made to overcome these problems. Whilst growing up close to one another, there are many opportunities for learning about each other, learning to work together and learning how to overcome difficulties both inside and outside the relationship.

For many people great friendships have been forged outside the family where mutual love, care, respect and support have grown. These relationships have been made from choice and remain through choice, there is always the freedom and opportunity to walk away if that is what is wanted. They are also not part of the family hierarchy, the in-fighting and pressures to conform, therefore each can know that the other is there because they feel that the relationship they have is important and of value.

Problems can happen to anyone at any time. When we suffer loss we all feel the pain of grief, but every loss means different things to different people. What hurts most to one will not be what hurts most to another. As we move along and meet many different people, some will only be in contact with us for a short while, perhaps while the grief is acute and until some balance is restored.

At different times we all need the support of different people, many of these will go their separate ways as situations change, maybe through a house move, a relative dying or the support of a different group is needed. But many of these will always remain as a light in our heart forever.

At all times but particularly at times of loss, whilst we are suffering from grief and travelling the road to recovery, it is whether we have love, support and care from others or not, that makes the difference. It affects the direction of our life, how well we cope with whatever life throws at us and at times whether or not we decide that living is in fact an option.

PART 4

SOME QUESTIONS FOR CONSIDERATION

We know how far we have travelled,
when we can consider the possibility
of gains as well as losses.

SOME QUESTIONS FOR CONSIDERATION

What has been lost?

When there is a bereavement without a death, at first it may not be so much a realisation of what we have lost, it is more likely to be a sense of our world crashing down and everything being shattered.

Often these things suddenly happen and matters are taken out of our control, perhaps someone is arrested, a diagnosis is given or a partner walks out. Although this is about them, is happening to them or being done by them it can feel like it is happening to you.

It can feel as though you are being stripped of more than everything. Your clothes making you exposed and unprotected. Your skin so that you are raw. Your insides so that you are empty. Your bones so that you can no longer stand. Your heart so that you have nothing left.

Usually it is the practical and material things that initially demand our attention and intrude into our thoughts and lives and which also push us into moving forward. Sometimes it is a matter of dealing with things that we can see and know how to do, all too often we have to do things that we do not or hardly know. Sometimes it is a matter of making decisions with little information and very little knowledge of the best thing to do or the likely outcome.

Just being able to see how you can possibly manage is often impossible, the enormity of it all seems too much to cope with and it can be very frightening. At first even the things that should be routine, such as washing and dressing, getting the kids to school or going to work may not be managed well. It often seems that no sooner have we moved a step forward than we are washed back by the waves of our grieving.

As we begin to come out of the numbness and shock, we begin to see what we have lost, what we believe we have lost and what we may still lose. We need to try to find what the reality is and the balance between, what we have to accept, what we do not have to accept and what is worth fighting for.

Many people face the same fights but each of us has to decide which if any of the battles we are going to take on. The fight may be to prove someone innocent, for a child's life, to keep your children with you or for maintenance payments.

Whether your fight is right or wrong, whether you succeed or not may not be known for a long time, if ever. It is for you to decide, even though there may be very few clues and little help. Others can only give their own personal views and opinions from how it looks to them, from where they are and what they think that they would do in the same situation.

So much belief, trust and peace of mind is lost, the belief that if you did things right, life would be fine, the belief that life is fair and just or that there are right answers.

For many people this is the first time that they have had to carry the full consequences of their decisions, faced the impact that their decisions will have on the lives of others as well as themselves and felt the aloneness that this creates. For others the decisions have been taken out of their hands, no matter what they say or do there is nothing that they can do, giving feelings of total helplessness, hopelessness and aloneness.

The losses are variable, they come in many different sizes and at different times. To some there is a loss of faith, another person may not have had this in the first place, there may be a loss of income, a home, a standard of living and material goods but for others there is little change in their material state. Some may lose the arguments, fights and in some cases the violence but it may be replaced with emptiness and loneliness.

Some people appear to float through all sorts of difficulties whilst others collapse at the least problem. Some may quietly and stoically plod through the pain and difficulties, dealing with each thing as it comes, whilst others appear to be in a permanent state of collapse. For many people it feels as though everything has been lost and there is no gain in trying further.

Just as everything is somewhat different to each person, so are the times when they grieve for their loss. Grieving may be immediate or it may be postponed for years. Initially there may be so much to do that there is no time to deal with our own grief and we have to put ourselves 'on hold'.

Grieving has so many parts and facets, it may be that we can deal with some but there are other things that we cannot get past or let go of. It may be that we feel that we should or we should not be behaving in a certain way and therefore refuse to work our way through a necessary part.

At times, moving on means that it is necessary to look at the future and face some of the 'what if's' the 'how will I cope?' and the 'I don't want this'. It is difficult to see how you will cope on your own or how you will ever trust anyone again; how you will cope when your child grows up; what you will do when they are released from prison or how you cope with the guilt of being relieved when they have died.

It is hardly surprising then that for many people the life they are living is shut off from their hopes for the future as well as their fears, for them their loss is a great part of their life. However much some people achieve in terms of material success it is at the loss of part of themselves, if it is shut away with their grief.

As we move on, we begin to realise that many of the things that we most dreaded and felt that we could not cope with, when they actually happened were not the problem or difficulty that we had expected. Often we come through these things feeling pleased and proud of ourselves. The things that really get to us are often the small things that we had not even considered.

We often forget or do not consider congratulating ourselves on the things that we have achieved, they may not be very big but each is a milestone and should at the very least be noted. We generally believe that the big things we face should just be taken in our stride, often believing that this is the way that everyone else manages. We beat ourselves up when we do not achieve the standard we expect of ourselves and generally behave in a way that we would not expect from anyone else.

There are also those who feel that they are unable to do anything for themselves or by themselves, they feel that life has given them a worse deal than anyone else and they expect to be rescued or have things done for them. To grow they must learn about what they have to do for themselves, what can be expected of others and what in fact they can manage to do.

Whilst we are not achieving things for ourselves or not seeing and appreciating what we are in fact achieving, we are not laying down the building blocks on which we grow, we are in this way preventing our own growth and thereby creating our own losses.

What do I have?

Lost in what we have lost and what we do not have, it is very easy to forget or not see what we have, that is, except for the things we have that we do not want.

As time passes, we start to realise what it is that we have really lost and the true value of it, both to ourselves and to others. For example, if we have lost a partner, we may realise that what we have lost is greater than we ever knew. The person meant more to us than we ever realised, it may be that they did so much for us that we do not even know how to function without them.

It may however be, that in their absence we begin to be aware that what we had was not good, the view we had was mistaken and in fact we did not have the life, help, support and care that we thought we had.

It may be that our baby has been diagnosed as having a learning disability. As the initial shock begins to recede we may realise that what we have is a baby, one who needs our love and care, at present that is all that matters, later will be the time to deal with the rest.

When we know and can accept that our child is gay, we can then have a real place in each other's lives.

Where there is bereavement without a death, much of our grief is caused by what we have rather than what we have lost. We have a changed life, probably one we did not want, in place of the person we knew, were expecting or thought we had, there is someone we do not know and probably do not want.

It usually means that we have gained a lot more work, together with many more appointments, a disturbed family to be settled and probably a lack of emotional or physical support.

It often feels as though everything that we have is what we do not want. We need to examine the situation to see what the reality is but this may feel far too frightening. If we look more closely at the situation, there is the possibility that we will see that nothing is safe or secure, there are more questions than answers and any answers that we can find, are not sure or definite.

From this very shaky position it is hard to really see what we have got and to believe that anything worthwhile can possibly come from it. Life can look different if it is looked at from a different direction and it is useful sometimes to look at some of the small things, the things that we often do not see.

When we feel that there is nothing good or worthwhile happening in our lives, it sometimes helps if we make a point of noting three nice things that happen each day. These things may be as little as someone smiling at you, a kind word, seeing a pretty flower or noticing that the sun shone. Although it may seem to be a pathetic exercise, when we start looking for the good things we realise that there is so much more than we expected and our spirits grow with our list.

When we look at what we have got we often believe that we have nothing, because what we really want is what we have lost and we believe that it is the only thing that will make us feel better. What we probably have is a lot of smaller things which we need to put together to begin to make a new life.

At the best of times we forget to appreciate what we have or to appreciate it in a positive manner, just as we do not feel like giving thanks for a nice warm bed when we have to get out into the cold. When we have been dealt a cruel blow it is even harder to see anything positive but if we can see and appreciating what we have, however small, we can begin to see that there are positive things that we can use as a base on which to build.

What can I do with it?

The hardest thing is perhaps not to try to answer this question immediately, most of us rush off and try to find the answer, as we crumple into a heap we demand that it is provided or we believe and insist that there is none.

In many cases we are unable to do anything initially. Generally what is happening is happening and there is very little we can do. What we often do not see, believe or feel is that we do in fact have the choice of staying in the situation or not, of doing what is needed or not. We are often faced with choices that people should not have to make, it often has more of the feeling of being between a rock and a hard place than a choice and any alternatives appear grim.

Often it is not until much later, with the benefit of hindsight, that we realise there were in fact more choices than we could see at the time but even here we have to realise that these would also have had their problems and their price.

People often say that they wish they had known more at the time, more of what the future held, more of what choices there were and what they could have done. But the other side of this coin is that if we knew what was ahead, how many of us would not have gone on?

It is important to be as informed as possible about what is available, what are the most likely outcomes, how have others in similar situation fared and how this relates to you and your situation. Even if you decide to reject all that you have heard or been offered at least the decision will be made from more of a position of strength and knowledge.

It is hardly surprising that we do not know what to do and how to cope in these situations, generally we were not brought up with anything like this or taught how to deal with it. For most people, dealing with the ups and downs of everyday life are enough of a challenge, at least with these we have the option of copying or rejecting what our parents did or looking at what our friends and neighbours do and comparing notes with them.

When something bad happens, all too often we are isolated and do not know anyone else in this position. It can take a long time for us to find others in the same boat as ourselves and often even longer to accept that this is the boat that we are in.

We are taken away from looking at ourselves as we spend our time considering what we can do with what we have. We try to avoid the possibility that the answer may be nothing or perhaps that it is not for us to do anything. Many find that they can make a positive difference by working with their child, fighting for justice, starting or being part of a group which supports, fund raises or lobby but these things can also lead to strain on both the individual and the family.

Often the hardest thing to do is to hand someone back their own life and give them responsibility for it or to pass this on to another, then look at ourselves and take on responsibility for ourselves, our own lives and those who are dependant on us. It is very often easier to run someone else's life, to know what they should do, how they should be and how to resolve their problems. Knowing what to do with our own is far more difficult and rarely carries the same feelings of certainty.

What we have changes with time, the fortunes of each of us go up and down, the babies that we have grow and change, the people in our lives come and go. There is nothing as certain as the fact that things will change, there are few answers for all time, what is right for us now will not be right for another person, time or place. We can only do the best that we can in any situation with the circumstances, energy and information we have at the time.

What can be gained?

Very often the first answer that springs to mind is 'nothing'. Often it will still be the answer after some consideration, probably because all we can see is the loss and we are aware that this cannot be re-gained.

We will have learned about some different things but this is a mixed blessing because there are many things that we would gladly un-know as we wish for the return of things to how they were. We have had some different experiences but very often these are experiences that we would not have chosen to have and we have gone through experiences that we would not have wished on our worst enemy.

Through the difficult times, through our pain and grief we have the opportunity to learn and grow, the opportunity to change the way we think, the way we see things and the way we live our lives. This is what we can gain, but we do not have to gain anything.

Everyone has the right to choose whether they want to gain anything from their experience and to grow from it. Each person has the right to hold on to their grief, anger and pain if this is what they feel is right for them and to move on, if and when they wish.

For each person the gains will be different, partly because of the person they are and partly because we gain what we wish to gain, these cannot be forced on anyone and each person will make a different choice.

There are many people, particularly those who have so far been onlookers, who believe that personal growth is an automatic and inevitable result of life's traumas. It is assumed that life's trials will automatically make those who are dealing with them stronger and more able to cope, even though they can see all those who have not yet learned, grown or become stronger.

It is often very hard for those looking on to see someone suffering, it is also hard to live with someone who appears to be hanging on to their grief and misery. It is hard not to tell someone to pull themselves together and make other such comments, it is very difficult to allow someone their grief and the time and space they need to deal with it, it is painful to remain alongside without judging. But they are not the only ones who are trying to cope with pain and difficulty, nor is the potential for growth confined to them. We cannot grow ourselves just by seeing the suffering of another or talking to them, it is only by being alongside, feeling and sharing that we are able to have this opportunity.

What we can gain is mostly what we strive to gain. There are many who feel that they have lost so much and suffered so much pain that in future they will concentrate on the material things in life as they feel these are safer, more secure and reliable. Others face great material losses but consider that their gains will be through personal growth.

Often the first difficulty is accepting that the gains that we can make are worth the effort and pain that are required. The gains that we can have are often not what we feel that we need or want, they are not what we were looking for and we could probably manage without them.

Very often the gains appear to be the very things that we have lost in our grief and we feel resentful that we have to work so hard just to go back to where we were. The truth of the matter is that we cannot go back to that place even if we wished to, we cannot un-know what we know, we cannot remove our experiences. The self-confidence that we can gain will not be the same as we had before, our appreciation of things is different, we can become stronger more accepting of others and more self-assured.

We may feel that our value systems were what they should be, we may pride ourselves on the fact that we are not materialistic but often it is not until we lose something that we realise how we value it. We may not be materialistic but we may for example, value academic ability highly. If this is so it will be difficult to value a learning disabled child as much as their brighter siblings.

If it is of great importance to us to see our children happily married and providing us with grandchildren, our personal value system will have to change for us to value the lifestyle of a homosexual child.

Whatever the changes we struggle to make, there will be great personal loss to be coped with. To deal with this it will be necessary to look at how and what we value in others and thereby we will be given the opportunity for change.

We may in fact find that we have changed our values very little but by looking at them with the eyes of our new experiences we can be more assured that what we value and the value systems we have are right for us and will serve us well.

There is a lot of knowledge and self-knowledge that we can gain, we learn that it is only when we die that we stop learning and it is only those who have died who stay the same. Therefore there is the potential for growth and change in all. We learn for example, that we cannot measure someone else's loss or compare it with our own or another. We see how easy and pointless it is to judge someone else and to use this as a measure of our own or another's success or failure.

As we grow we become stronger. This can be quite frightening, we may feel that we do not want to be stronger, that if we do we may crack or we may end up carrying the world. However, the strength that we can gain is quiet and gentle, it can give us the confidence to say no, the confidence to know that we can cope, to take control of our own life and allow others to do the same with theirs.

We can also gain the confidence, hope and optimism that will enable us to pick up the pieces and move on, however long it takes.